North West Railway Walks

—

An Explorer's Guide to the Lost Railways of the South Pennines and Surrounding Hills

Robin H. Martin

Sigma Leisure, Wilmslow

First published in 1990 by

Sigma Leisure, an imprint of

Sigma Press, 1 South Oak Lane, Wilmslow, SK9 6AR, England.

British Library Cataloguing in Publication Data

A CIP catalogue record for this book is available from the British Library.

ISBN: 1-85058-215-7

Typesetting and design by

Sigma Hi-Tech Services Ltd

Printed by:

Manchester Free Press

Maps drawn by: Pam Upchurch

Cover Photograph: High in the hills above the Goyt Valley, walkers follow the old Cromford and High Peak railway; the reservoir in the middle distance supplied water to the winding engine for the inclined plane leading down to Errwood. *Photograph by Graham Beech*

Contents

Acknowledgements

The author would like to express his special thanks to the Chief Librarian of Rawtenstall Library, the Librarian of Bacup Library, Basil Jeuda, D. Ripley and Harold Bowtell for permission to reproduce the historical photographs from their collections in this book. Some of the photographs have already appeared in publications from Oakwood Press and I am grateful for their permission to reproduce them here. The author's thanks are also owed to Mrs. H. Pilling for the loan of a high class camera for the taking of the other photographs, and to Graham Beech for the cover photograph.

The author owes a great debt of gratitude to those authors who researched and had published material on the railways covered by the walks in this book. Among these special mention must be made of Harold Bowtell who very kindly gave the author some further information from his researches on some of the reservoir railways in areas not yet covered in his three books already published. The third and most recent of these, 'Lesser Railways of Bowland Forest and Craven Country', will be of interest to users of this book who, having had their interest in reservoir railways stimulated, may wish to explore further afield.

Hill Railways – an introduction

Narrow gauge and light railways which run in our hills have a fascination and an allurement which puts them apart from railways which run or ran in the flatter areas of our island. Their ascents and descents, their sharp twists and turns following contours place them in a different category from those railways which, while running through our hills, blast their way through and cut ruthlessly into the hills in deep cuttings or long tunnels, crossing deep· valleys or gorges on high embankments or massive stone viaducts in an almost straight line. The hill railway of the light standard gauge or narrow gauge variety will, on the contrary, pay much more respect to its surroundings by bending with the contour and following the slope more closely, only occasionally and sparingly using the device of cutting, tunnel or embankment to shorten the way. The hill railway would often weave up some remote valley or climb some wild hill which no 'heavy' railway would have dreamed of touching.

Most of the hill railways have long since closed but, because they traversed land not attractive to the modern plough, their earthworks, light though they be, have often been left untouched. Indeed, there is often more left of some hill railway long since abandoned than of some 'Beeching-axed' lowland line travelled on by people within recent memory. Often, in regard to the latter, those lines which ran in intensively farmed areas have left virtually no trace of their existence. Even in the less flat areas embankments are removed and cuttings filled in at an alarming rate. Fortunately, however, many of our hill railways have so far managed to escape that nightmare of the railway archaeologist, namely, landscaping, redevelopment and land reclamation.

The object of this book is to act as a guide to those who feel they would like to explore on foot some, at least of the fascinating hill railways of the southern Pennines and surrounding hills. The hill railways explored by these walks fall into three groups.

In the first group are some railways which had short but very busy lives in the first half of this century. These were the railways built to service work in connection with the construction of reservoirs situated deep in the heart of the southern Pennines. Some of these lines ran for several miles and had sizeable studs of steam locomotives.

In the second group are those railways whose basic traffic, even if not always planned as such, was the transport of lime and limestone from quarries in the limestone hills of north Derbyshire and north Staffordshire. Some of these railways, as will be seen, have origins going right back to the early days of railway history. Unlike the railways in the first group, many of these 'limestone' railways lasted a very long time.

In the third group are a series of railways, of both narrow and standard gauge, which climbed high up into that outlier of the Pennine Hills centred on Rossendale in order to transport building stone from often quite remote stone quarries down into the heavily industrialised valleys below.

By no means all of the railways in the above three groups are covered in this book. Those that have been selected for exploration by foot are those which the author feels are either the most interesting or the most readily accessible in each group.

For the exploration of the remains of these railways 18 walks are outlined. Some railways are covered by two or more walks which can be combined, if so desired, into longer walks. Each suggested excursion takes you on a circular walk designed to be enjoyable and attractive to the general walker as well as of interest to the railway enthusiast. The lengths of the walks vary but even the longest should not take more than a good half day.

All routes are on public rights of way or over paths freely used by the public at the time of writing. No route is over any private land where any notice, gate or fence has been erected to deter trespass. Indeed readers are requested, however tempting it might be, to avoid walking on the course of any railway where he or she would be regarded as a trespasser.

The walks suggested are not on the courses of railways but on footpaths, bridleways, old tracks and lanes near the course of some abandoned hill railway in order to observe its remains. However, there are some abandoned hill railways which have trackbeds over part of which, at least, public rights of way have been registered. Where this is so the walk will, naturally, be on the course of the railway itself.

Some Practical Points

While every effort has been made to accurately record essential features, you should be aware that things can change very quickly on the ground. New fences can appear and others disappear; a stile can be changed into a gate or vice versa. Worst of all, bulldozers can quickly alter even major features and sometimes the odd awkward landowner obstructs a public right of way. In the case of the latter, having checked that you are on a right of way and that the path has not been diverted, inform either the Ramblers' Association or the local council of the position and nature of the obstruction. Don't forget, however, that paths are often legally diverted or closed. Unfortunately, often there is no permanent signposting of these diversions or closures.

Many would say summer is the time to do the walks, but winter and early spring could be considered by some to be the best time. It is then that trees and bushes are free of foliage and the grass low, allowing features to be seen which can often be hidden in the warmer months of the year. Some features pointed out in the text are certainly not visible when leaves abound.

A sketch map is provided for each walk showing features intended to guide you both in finding your way and to point out the observable remains of the railway explored. Use the appropriate Ordnance Survey map, preferably the Path-finder series, as a supplement to the sketch maps.

The type of footwear will vary both between walks and when the walk is undertaken but generally speaking after wet weather or in winter waterproof footwear is recommended on all walks.

Binoculars can be very useful for viewing some interesting railway feature which cannot be closely approached because it is on private property.

Imperial measurements are used mainly because the books and maps referred to by the author are in this measure. On the walks yards are used only as an approximation. As a metre is only slightly more than a yard, conversion to metres should not be difficult. Each sketch map has an approximate scale in both measures.

The word 'tramway' in this book always indicates a light standard or narrow gauge railway and never, of course, an electric street tramway. The use of the word in the former sense was common in Victorian times. The terms 'railway' and 'tramway' are virtually interchangeable as far as the lines covered in this book are concerned. For instance, with regard to the quarry lines of East Rossendale (Walk 17) the O.S. map of 1891 labels them as 'tramways' while the O.S. map of 1909 labels the same lines 'railways'.

Some walks are in part on exposed moorland. On these walks hill railway explorers are strongly advised to take the following precautions:

● Leave details of the walk being followed with someone not on the walk.

● Take some food and drink including emergency rations.

● Give yourself plenty of time.

● However fine the day at the start of the walk, always carry waterproof clothing.

● Take a map, compass, torch, whistle. (The international distress signal is six long blasts or flashes at ten second intervals followed by a pause of one minute).

On all walks a compass is useful as directions are often given using the sixteenfold division of the compass. Familiarity with these divisions (north north west, north west, west north west, etc.) will be useful for the user of this book.

Make sure you know how to use a map and compass on moorland in poor visibility. The 'Silva' type compass with its specially marked clear plastic baseplate is the easiest to use with a map. In poor visibility the procedure using this sort of compass is to place the baseplate edge on the map connecting the point where you believe you are with the point you are making for. Then turn the dial till the orienting lines on the dial are parallel with the north/south grid lines of the map. Next turn the compass together with the map underneath until the red end of the magnetic needle points to north. Move forward aiming for some visible feature (clump of grass, mound, etc.) that lies along the mark indicated by the arrow at the bottom of the baseplate. Repeat the procedure till you are clear of the cloud or fog.

Suggestions for Further Reading and Bibliography

The amount and quality of published material on the railways covered by the walks in this book varies widely. Most of the reservoir railways are fully covered by Harold Bowtell's two excellent books dealing with the subject. The Cromford and High Peak Railway and the Peak Forest Tramway both have a book or books entirely devoted to them. As for the rest, one has to collect information from a variety of published and sometimes unpublished sources. The following are the main works consulted by the author.

Walks 1, 2 and 3

'Reservoir Railways of the Yorkshire Pennines' by Harold D. Bowtell, Oakwood Press, 1979.

Walk 4

'Saddleworth Visitor Guide', Oldham Metropolitan Borough, 1986.

Bulletin of the Saddleworth Historical Society (scattered references in a number of issues).

The Minutes of the Ashton, Stalybridge and Dukinfield Waterworks Committee.

Walks 5 and 6

'The Peak Forest Tramway' by D. Ripley, Locomotion Papers No.38, Oakwood Press, 1972.

The Railway Magazine, September 1963. Article by P. Clowes.

'Great Central' by George Dow, Vol. 1, Locomotive Publishing Company, 1959.

Walk 7 (Fernilee Reservoir part)

'Reservoir Railways of Manchester and the Peak' by Harold D. Bowtell, Oakwood Press, 1977.

Walks 7 to 10

'The Cromford and High Peak Railway' by A. Rimmer, Locomotion Paper No.10, Oakwood Press.

'The Cromford and High Peak Railway' by John Marshall, David & Charles.

'A Regional History of the Railways of Great Britain'. Vol.7: 'The West Midlands' by Rex Christiansen, David & Charles.

The Railway Magazine, January 1961. Article by W.H. Hoult, 'Fell's Experimental Railway in Derbyshire'.

Walks 11 and 12

'The Canals of the West Midlands' by Charles Hadfield, David & Charles.

'The Trent and Mersey Canal' by Jean Lindsay, David & Charles.

'Railways in the Peak District' by C.P. Nicholson and Peter Barnes, Dalesman.

'Stone Blocks and Iron Rails' by Bertram Baxter, David & Charles .

'The Caldon Canal and Tramroad' by Peter Lead, Locomotion Paper No. 116, Oakwood Press.

Walks 13 to 18

'Railways and Mineral Tramways of Rossendale' by B. Roberts, Locomotion Papers No. 76, Oakwood Press.

'Quarrying in Rossendale' by J. Davies (unpublished work in Rawtenstall and Bacup Libraries).

'Mr. Pilling's Short Cut to China' by Chris Aspin, Helmshore Local History Society.

'The Bacup Branch' (No.3 in series on branch lines of the Lancashire and Yorkshire Railway), Lancashire and Yorkshire Railway Society.

'The Changing Faces of Rossendale: Building Blocks' by Denis Revell, Rossendale Countryside and Tourism Interpretive Project.

Location Map

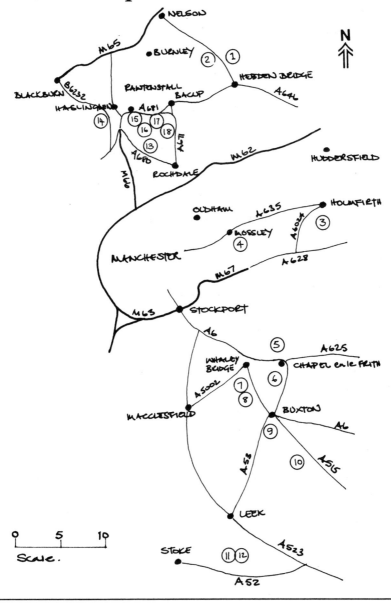

Key

– – ▶ – – –	route of work
–·–· ▶·· – ·–	alternative route
—·—·—·—	standard gauge railway (operational)
— · — · —·—	standard gauge railway (non-operational)
┼┼┼┼┼ ┼┼┼┼ + + + + + + ———————	narrow gauge and light standard gauge railways
∼∼∼∼◯	river/reservoirs
══════—	roads
▰	buildings
∴∴┽┼┼┼—	puddle clay field
┴┴┴┴┴┴┴	canal
R.T.	where walk follows railway track

Walk 1: The Walshaw Dean Railway

Map: Pathfinder Maps 681 SD 83/93 and 690 SD 82/92 or Outdoor Leisure Map 21 'South Pennines'

Distance: just over 6 miles

Start: The National Trust car park above Clough Hole, Hardcastle Crags on the Hebden Bridge to Nelson and Colne road. Grid reference SD 969 298.

By Car: Turn northwards off the A646 Todmorden to Halifax road just over a $1/4$ mile west of the centre of Hebden Bridge onto the road to Heptonstall. After a $1/4$ mile climb up a steep hill, at the fork take the right hand road to Slack. Through the village of Slack at the west end, go off to your right onto the road to Nelson and Colne. The car park is on the right in just under a mile.

By Public Transport: There is a frequent train service to Hebden Bridge from Manchester and Leeds. At times buses from Hebden Bridge to Slack just a mile away from the start of the walk.

This walk explores the upper section of what was, perhaps, the most interesting of all the reservoir railways of the Pennine Hills. The outer section of the walk, closely following the course of the railway, is on footpaths running above Hebden Water and Alcomden Water. The return section goes over the moor to just over 1,300 feet above sea-level but there are no steep climbs. The return section is on a permissive path which is closed on certain days during the grouse shooting season. As with other moorland walks, a clear day is preferable.

The Railway

This three-foot gauge line was built by Enoch Tempest who in 1900 contracted to build for Halifax Corporation a chain of three large reservoirs at Walshaw Dean north of Hardcastle Crags near Hebden Bridge. The line began not, as one might expect, at Hebden Bridge Station but at a point high up on the valley side in a field just north of the village of Heptonstall. Here the depot was sited from where the line launched out. This depot was officially known as Whitehall Nook but soon acquired the illuminating name of 'Dawson City'.

Construction of the line began in October 1900. The railway's course ran westwards and then northwards and then again westwards, all the time keeping to the lip of the deep clough above Hebden Water. After about two-and-a-half miles the line crossed the clough on an impressive wooden trestle viaduct which was not completed until May 1901. The line then continued on for about a mile up the east side of the valley as far as the site of the first reservoir which was reached on 12 June 1901. Soon the railway was extended another mile further up the valley to the site of the wall of the top reservoir which was situated about four-and-a-half miles from the depot at 'Dawson City'. Besides the usual sidings and short branches around the construction sites, a mile long branch, which left the 'main line' at the site of the middle dam, ran along the west side of the valley to the puddle clayfield. The railway also served several stone quarries, the most important of which was Hell Holes Quarry about half a mile east of the trestle viaduct and situated in what is now the Hardcastle Crags National Trust land.

In all 15 locomotives are known to have worked on the line. With the exception of an 0-6-0 saddle tank called 'Tenacity', all the engines were 0-4-0 saddle tanks. Two of the engines were built by Hunslet and the rest by W.G. Bagnall. One of the engines called 'Esau' was later at work on the Scout Moor Quarries line (see Walk 13). All these locomotives had to be hauled up over 300 feet from Hebden Bridge Station to the depot at 'Dawson City' by steam lorry or by teams of horses.

Besides the expected stone and clay carrying wagons, the railway possessed no less than 15 workmen's coaches which were former Liverpool horse tramcars regauged to three feet. At the peak of the workings three 'Paddy Mails' or workmen's passenger trains left 'Dawson City' at ten minute intervals from 5.30 in the morning onwards. Some passenger trains were propelled by two locomotives, one at the front and one at the rear. The coaches apparently still bore their old destination boards so one had cars trundling into the heart of the Yorkshire Moors bearing indications such as 'Fazakerley' and 'Lime Street'.

The operation of the railway was not without a number of accidents which sadly included the death of an engine driver. This occurred when his engine turned over while propelling wagons over a wooden bridge between the reservoir sides. A worse tragedy was narrowly avoided when the 'Dawson City Mail', on its homeward run on the evening of 12 August 1912 and pulled by the locomotive 'Esau', came off the rails at Clough Hole roughly halfway between the viaduct and the southern terminus. A plunge into the steep clough below was avoided only by a sycamore tree being in the way.

The trestle bridge at Blake Dean (near point 5 of the walk) looking upstream. A 'Paddy Mill' train crosses the bridge on its way back to 'Dawson City'. *Reproduced by kind permission from The Harold Bowtell Collection.*

The railway had a much longer life than expected. Originally only four years were allowed for the building of the reservoirs. The opening ceremony for the three reservoirs was, in fact, held on 1 October 1907 but attempts to overcome problems connected with leakage caused the section of the railway as far as Lipscomb Road about half a mile south of the lower reservoir to be retained and a temporary railhead established at the latter point. Finally, however, the work was completed and the railway was no longer needed. The demolition of the trestle viaduct began on 14 August 1912. By June of the following year the whole route of the main line where it passed over fields had been reinstated and the stone walls through which it passed rebuilt. Because of this reinstatement there is almost nothing left of the first two miles of the line but of the rest of the railway much interesting visual evidence still remains. It is this upper section of the line that the walk will explore.

Because its course is crossed at two points on the walk a brief mention ought to be made here of the Widdop Reservoir Tramway.

This horse worked tramway was built in 1872/73 to service the construction of Widdop Reservoir which is situated to the west of Walshaw Dean in the valley of Graining Water. It is believed to have been of three-foot gauge. It started at New Bridge Depot situated about a quarter of a mile north of the gates of the Hardcastle Crags estate or possibly even at the gates themselves. From New Bridge Depot the wagons were hauled up a very steep incline with a gradient of about 1 in 2.3 on special trucks which had larger wheels at the lower end so that the tramway wagons could be kept level. From the top of the incline the tramway went west then north and then west again, running parallel to but somewhat below the unmetalled road linking the hamlets of Walshaw and Shackleton to Holme Ends. At Holme Ends the tramway crossed the Alcomden Water and then appears to have struck directly across the moor to the west after which it passed down into the valley of Graining Water to reach the construction site of the reservoir at Widdop. The work of this reservoir, which was also for Halifax Corporation, was completed in 1878.

The Walk

[1] Before setting off from the car park look towards the south east to glimpse the start of the Walshaw Dean Reservoirs Railway. The starting point, 'Dawson City', was sited at the top of the spur which lies just to the right of a tall chimney you should be able to spot in the far distance on the other side of the valley. From here the railway ran immediately above the lip or sharp edge of the clough, just above the top of the woods. It bore round to the north through the bottom of the field in which the car park is situated. Because of reinstatement to agricultural

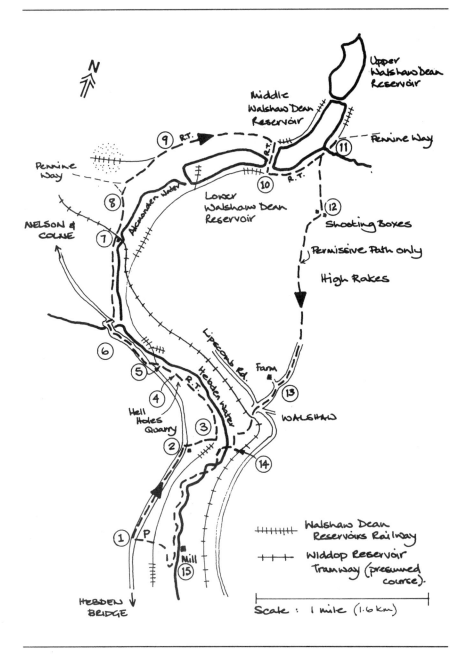

use of the track bed after closure in this section, the railway has left virtually no trace at all except for the hint of wall rebuilding where its course passed through the numerous stone walls running down the upper gentle slope of the valley.

Go out of the car park onto the tarred road, turn right and make your way northwards. On your right the course of the railway continued to run just above the woods, except for a short section just south east of the house ahead on your right where it ran through a short bit of the woods which juts a little further out to the west than the rest of the woods.

[2] Continue on the road until you get level with this first house on your right. Here take the path (public footpath sign) that leads eastwards off the road to the right of the barn lying north west of the house and bordering the road. Next go left through the gate immediately below the barn and then go diagonally across the yard to a second gate which opens into a field. The path continues on downhill running diagonally across this field. It passes through an iron fence and continues in a straight line across a second field until it comes up to a stone wall running straight downhill. Here continue on downhill keeping this wall on your left.

Halfway down note that a short section of this wall is made of better stones than the rest. This marks the point where the Walshaw Dean Railway passed through on its way up the valley.

[3] At the bottom of the fields go through the gap stile and descend to the trackway running parallel to the woodland boundary wall. Turn left on the trackway and proceed northwards. At first the trackway runs a little below the boundary wall but soon moves up to run immediately below it.

At the point where the trackway and boundary wall meet the trackway joins the railway trackbed, the railway having come across the field on your left obliquely crossing through the wall. Again note the change of stone in the wall with a straight joint marking the end of one section of rebuilding after the lifting of the railway. Proceed along the trackway as it continues in a north westerly direction running now directly on the trackbed of the Walshaw Dean Railway.

Soon the track bends round to the left through a wide cutting. Perhaps there were some sidings here. The trackway ends here and the course of the railway is marked now by a footpath only. Soon the path drops down into and then climbs out again of a small depression which the railway would have crossed by a wooden trestle bridge. On the other side of this depression the footpath regains the railway trackbed which continues in a westerly direction in a shallow single rail track cutting.

[4] Soon the trackbed widens and on your left the sizeable quarry of Hell Holes comes into view. One can imagine the scene of activity here with busy little steam engines shunting wagons loaded with stone into trains ready for the journey up to the site of reservoirs. Continue on the path as it leaves the quarry and the woods behind, following the railway trackbed which is now terraced out on the steep slope above Hebden Water. Soon another gully is crossed which again the railway would have crossed on a wooden trestle bridge.

[5] Before long the trackbed widens and then suddenly fades out. Here the railway turned right to cross the ravine by a large wooden trestle viaduct. The concrete footings for this impressive structure can still be seen in the valley bottom. The course of the .railway is visible on the opposite side of the valley. The main line can be clearly seen sweeping off to the west climbing slightly and bending round through a shallow cutting as it starts to turn to the north to climb up to the reservoirs. You can also see the course of a siding of some length going off to the east to end at what appears to have been a small quarry.

Proceed now along the path which continues straight on in a westerly direction along the side of the valley until you come to the Hebden Bridge-Colne road. Go along the road down to the stone bridge to cross Graining Water.

[6] To get the best views of the railway avoid the temptation to use the path in the valley bottom. Instead proceed a little further along the tarred road as it climbs turning first to the left and then sharply to the right passing above an old graveyard. Just above the graveyard the road turns sharp left again. Here leave the road making your way through a gap stile on the right-hand side of the bend in the corner.

On the opposite side of the valley of the Alcomden Water, to the east of you, the course of the railway can be clearly seen again as it clings to the top lip of the clough climbing steadily northwards towards the reservoirs.

Having passed through the gap stile, immediately turn sharp left crossing the foundations of an old wall. Proceed north north west. After some yards a cemented trackway appears below you on your right. The path goes straight on moving a little away from the stone wall on your left to join the cement trackway at an oblique angle further on.

At the point where the path joins the cement trackway a glance at the other side of the valley will reveal what appears to be a long siding leaving the main line and dropping down in a northerly direction to the valley bottom. This is, in fact, the route of the horse tramway to Widdop Reservoir situated over the moor to the west (see the introduction to this walk). It has been suggested that in the final days of the Walshaw Dean Railway a siding was laid on this section of the old tramway trackbed in order to get to a temporary railhead at Lipscomb Road.

[7] Continue on along the cement trackway for about a quarter of a mile until you come to a stone barn on your right.

The Widdop Reservoir tramway appears to have crossed over the river somewhere near the bridge below and to have continued westwards, passing immediately north of the barn and continuing on up the hill on your left. Just the other side of the wooden kissing gate what could be some traces of its course can be observed.

Proceed along the cement trackway as it climbs gently to the north west.

On the other side of the valley the course of the Walshaw Dean Railway can be seen approximately halfway up the slope running northwards until it comes to a stone wall. North of this wall the railway continued to climb steadily up the valley side to reach a point level with the west end of the retaining wall of the lower reservoir. Alas, however, 'reinstatement' has completely obliterated any trace of the course of this section of the railway.

[8] Continue along the cement trackway until you come to a fork. Here take the right-hand track (the yellow arrow route). Another track soon comes in on the left. Here you have joined the Pennine Way. Continue on along the trackway as it proceeds northwards.

On your left you will notice a plantation of fir trees. This plantation marks the site of the Baiting House puddle clayfield which was opened up in June 1905 when the first puddle clayfield 'by Turners Farm', just below the site of the lower reservoir wall, was exhausted. The puddle field was served by a branch line of the Walshaw Dean Railway. This line ran from the puddle field along the north west side to the valley to a point level with the top of the north end of the wall of the middle dam. This puddle field line 'joined' the cement trackway you are on at the point where there is a metal gate on your left just level with the north tip of the plantation. From this point onwards the cement trackway is on the course of the railway.

Continue on north eastwards on this trackway.

[9] As you draw level with Lower Walshaw Dean Reservoir, you will once again be able to pick out the course of the main line of the Walshaw Dean Railway as it continues on its way up the valley. It is clearly visible as it bends away from the lower reservoir to curve uphill towards the top of the middle reservoir.

Continue on along the concrete trackway (still, of course, on the trackbed of the puddle field branch) as it goes gently downhill through a shallow cutting and over an embankment to pass round the north side of the reservoir keeper's stone house (completed in 1905). Follow the Pennine Way signs pointing across the retaining wall of the middle reservoir.

Halfway across it is worth stopping to note the remains of a quarry, now only just above the water level, on the west side of the lower reservoir. A branch line led from the main line on the east side, crossing over the valley on a trestle bridge to reach this quarry. To the north of you the course of the puddle field branch railway can be seen weaving its way above the west side of the middle reservoir making for the top reservoir. There was also at one time a link across the valley on the retaining wall of the middle reservoir according to the map in Harold Bowtell's book on this railway.

[10] At the end of the middle reservoir wall turn left, following the Pennine Way signs.

The path here, as it runs beside a by-wash channel, is on the course of the last section of the Walshaw Dean Railway as it made its way to its final destination at the site of the works connected with the construction of the upper reservoir.

Follow the Pennine Way as it passes through a stone wall and turns left onto a trackway to cross a stone bridge.

[11] Continue on the trackway until after a short climb you have a good view of Upper Walshaw Dean Reservoir where the railway ended somewhere at the base of what is now the retaining wall. On the opposite side the course of the puddle field branch can be seen running up to the same destination. So here ended this remarkable if somewhat temporary railway well up over a thousand feet in the Pennine Hills.

Make your way back along the trackway to just south of the stone bridge. The suggested route back, which leaves the Pennine Way here, is on a permissive path over land belonging to the Saville Estate and is liable to be closed to the public on grouse shooting days, in which case you will have to return by the way you came. The path, which runs over the moor to the hamlet of Walshaw, can be wet underfoot at times but does not involve any steep climbs.

To pick up the return route path, instead of following the Pennine Way path as it turns right through the stone wall, keep straight on along the rough trackway which, after going through a metal gate, makes its way up the hillside to the south west to end at two shooting huts.

[12] After passing between the two huts, bear right (a notice points you to the 'Crags') and follow the well used footpath over High Rakes.

Once over the top of the moor make for the left side of a thick clump of fir trees visible half-way down the hill. Where the open moor ends a stile gives access to a green lane which passes to the left of the fir trees and bears slightly right as it goes downhill.

[13] Near the farm, which appears on your right, go through the gate on the right where a stone wall juts out a little across the track. A few paces further on you meet a farm road. Bear left here and follow the farm road downhill until you come to the hamlet of Walshaw.

At Walshaw go straight over the east-west road (Lipscomb Road) and down to the bottom of the green ahead of you. Here go over the stile in the wall on your left and turn right. Go through the gate ahead of you and make your way down the slope, aiming for a section of wall jutting out from the boundary wall of the wood below.

It was somewhere here that the Widdop Reservoir horse tramway passed as it followed the contour but it has left no trace.

Follow the section of wall that runs downhill until, at the point where it turns right, you see a small wicket gate. Go through this gate, turn left and, after a few paces, turn sharp right and follow the path leading downhill above the north edge of Rowsham Clough.

[14] At the bottom turn left on the trackway, cross over the bridge and then turn right, making for the footbridge over Hebden Water. Having crossed over the footbridge, turn left and follow the well used path next to the river until you come to the old cotton mill at Gibson Wood Bridge, about three-quarters of a mile further on.

[15] After passing the mill, keep to the west side of the river and make your way up the trackway that leads to the south climbing steadily up the side of the valley. Keep to the trackway as, (halfway up), it bends sharp right, climbing now in a northerly direction. At the top of the wood the track emerges on to a field. It was somewhere here that the Walshaw Dean Railway crossed over the small clough on a trestle bridge.

At the top of the field is the car park where the walk began.

Walk 2: The Gorple Reservoirs Railway

Map: Pathfinder Map 681 SD83/93 or Outdoor Leisure Map 21'South Pennines'

Distance: About 6 miles

Start: Roadside car parking space approximately 4 miles from Hebden Bridge on the Hebden Bridge - Nelson/Colne road, about 600 yards east of the bridge over Graining Water. Grid reference SD 964 312.

By Car: Follow the same directions as for Walk 1 till you reach the National Trust Car Park above Clough Hole. From the car park continue on along the road for another mile. The parking space is opposite the point where the road widens on its south side by the entrance to the private road leading to Lower Gorple Reservoir Reservoir. There is a National Trust sign on the north side of the road near the parking space.

By Public Transport: The nearest bus stop is at Slack, 2 miles to the south east.

This walk in a remote section of the moors of the South Pennines near the watershed of our island explores the interesting remains of quite an extensive reservoir railway system. About half of the walk is on rough moor which can be very wet at times, so hiking boots are strongly recommended. There are no steep climbs but the walk does take you up to 1,250 feet above sea-level so days with low cloud are to be avoided.

The Railway

In June of 1927 the tender of Lehane, Mackenzie and Shand Ltd., was accepted by Halifax Corporation to build two reservoirs in a subsidiary valley of the Graining Water west of Hardcastle Crags and south of Widdop Reservoir (built almost half a century earlier). A three-foot gauge railway system was constructed by the contractors to service the construction work. The railway was barely two miles long between the two farthest points but, with branches taken into account, the system of 'permanent' lines came to about four miles of track in all.

The railway, of course, lasted only so long as the reservoirs were in building. The first sod of the work was cut on 14 July 1927 and the opening ceremony was performed on 7 June 1934. In its short life, however, the Gorple Reservoirs Railway was a very busy system with no less than 14 locomotives, all steam, known to have worked on it. These consisted of two 0-6-0 tank (one side and one saddle), three 0-4-0 well tank and nine 0-4-0 saddle tank locomotives. Of these no less than seven had worked on the Brownhill Reservoir Railway (see Walk 3).

The railway brought stone from two quarries at either end of the system and from one quarry up on the hillside to the reservoir workings. The latter quarry was served by what has been called a 'loco worked incline', while a self-acting, double track incline served the puddle clay field on the same hillside. Besides the normal stone and clay traffic to the work sites at both of the dams, the railway ran a 'mail' train for workmen from the eastern end of the system where the huts were situated to the 'top deck', as the navvies called the embankment of the upper reservoir. This train consisted of three open coaches of the toastrack type. There was even a 'glass coach' with platforms at both

High above the site of Lower Gorple Reservoir a six wheeled engine waits patiently while its trucks are loaded with clay from the puddle field. *Reproduced by kind permission of the Harold Bowtell Collection.*

ends and cushioned seats to convey councillors and their guests around the works.

From 1932 onwards till the official opening the Gorple Reservoirs in June 1934, the rail system was gradually run down and all 14 locomotives, with one possible exception, were transferred to the same contractor's work at Fernilee Reservoir in Derbyshire (see Walk 7).

The Walk

Several engines fuss around while workers 'puddle' the trench of Upper Gorple Reservoir. View from point 8 on the walk. *Reproduced by kind permission from The Harold Bowtell Collection.*

[1] Make your way westwards on the tarmac road down to the bridge over Graining Water. Follow the road as it goes over the bridge and turns to climb the hill on the north side of the valley.

[2] Where the road makes a sharp right-hand bend you will see, on your left side in the crook of the bend, a kissing gate (footpath sign). Go through this and take the path that leads westwards running at first with a stone wall on the left. Soon you are on open hillside. Keep

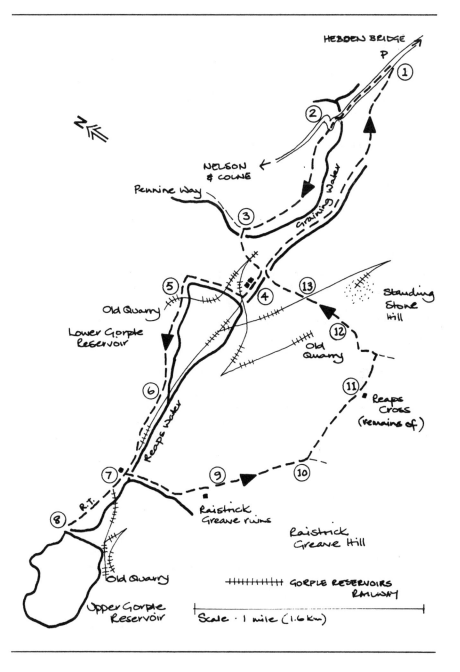

straight on, gradually climbing to the top of the valley side. Lower Gorple Reservoir soon comes into view and a tumbled stone wall appears on your right. Keep to the left of this wall as it runs along the lip of the valley roughly in a west north westerly direction.

Below you on the other side of the valley a quarry appears. Above this quarry the Gorple Reservoirs Railway reached its farthest point to the east. The stone would, presumably, have been lifted up by crane and loaded into wagons waiting at the top of the quarry.

[3] When you get opposite the quarry make your way down the slope, aiming for the first of the two wooden footbridges that appear below. Cross over the low wire fence just to the left of the first bridge. You are now on the Pennine Way which here runs on an old pack horse way. Cross both bridges and make your way up the hill on the south side valley on the stone slabbed way.

Once over the lip of the clough the path takes a straight route to the south. Soon you cross the trackbed of one of the two lines of the reservoir railway linking the quarry to the works. This line ran to the west on the level disappearing under what is the retaining wall of Lower Gorple reservoir. Almost immediately you cross the trackbed of the second line from the quarry. This also goes to the west but climbs steeply uphill. Note the little cutting away to your right.

[4] Continue on the path until you come to a concrete paved road. Turn right on this road which is owned by the Yorkshire Water Authority. There is no right of way over it but the public are allowed to use it. Pass the houses and workshops on your right until you come to the reservoir embankment. The upper line from the quarry crossed over here to the locomotive sheds and workshops which were just over the wall immediately south west of the embankment. From here the 'main line' moved up the valley in the middle of the area now filled by the reservoir, while another line climbed up through what is now a big rough pasture field to the south of the reservoir to a reversal neck. From here it climbed south eastwards to the stone quarry well up on the hillside. There is, however, not much direct evidence of the railway's existence to be seen from this point.

Cross the reservoir retaining wall on the concrete road. Near the other side you will have a good overall view of the trackbeds of the different lines immediately below the reservoir embankment. At the north end of the retaining wall turn left and follow the road on the north side of the reservoir.

[5] You will soon notice a large excavation on your right with the remains of what appears to have been a shallow cutting leading down to the rest of the railway system. Presumably there was a railway in this cutting, though none is shown here on the appropriate map in 'Reservoir Railways of the Yorkshire Pennines'.

Upper Gorple Reservoir viewed across the still waters of the lower reservoir. The course of the reservoir railway rises just to the right of the clough in the middle of the picture.

On the opposite side of the reservoir you should, with the aid of binoculars, be able to pick out the course of the double track incline that led from the puddle clay field high up on the hillside to the south east of the southern end of the reservoir retaining wall to a point now covered by water to the west of the retaining wall. It is more obvious at certain angles of observation than others, so if you do not spot it at first, try again as you go further along. Be careful not to confuse it with an old trackway which runs roughly parallel to the incline and to the west of it. The locomotive worked incline up to the quarry is even more difficult to make out. In mid-winter what could be some low earthworks of the trackbed near the reversal neck can be made out, just to the east of the fence running uphill from the middle of the south shore of the reservoir. The quarry tip for which the railway was making for is, however, clearly visible at the top of the rush filled slope above the south end of the reservoir embankment.

[6] Continue westwards along the concrete road until it bends a little to the right after coming level with the narrow western tongue of the reservoir. Here, if you look over the side of the road on your left, you should be able to make out the course of the 'main line' as it emerges out of the reservoir, climbing steeply to join the course of the concrete road just before the plantation of larch trees ahead on the left.

[7] Further on along the road, just after you have passed a large wooden hut on your right, a plantation of fir trees on the south side of the road comes into sight. Just before this plantation, on the other side of the clough, you can see the stone abutment of the trestle bridge which carried one branch of the railway to the upper reservoir over Reaps Water. Beyond the bridge the railway ran through a short cutting and then on a terrace above the side of the clough, both of which can be clearly seen. The other branch of the railway continued up to the reservoir roughly on the same course as the road on the north side of the clough.

[8] Follow the road to the top of the retaining wall of Upper Gorple Reservoir. Across on the other side, a little to the west of the southern end of the reservoir embankment, the quarry which was the farthest point west reached by the railway can be seen. You will see the southern branch below on the east side, disappearing into the reservoir embankment. Presumably it carried on climbing up the slope until it reached the quarry, but of this latter part nothing is clear now.

It seems likely that the upper part of the quarry was served by a separate railway which reached it by a double reversal. The appropriate map in 'Reservoir Railways of the Yorkshire Pennines' does not show a railway here but earthworks of what is likely to have been a railway trackbed can be seen leading away from the 'main line' of the southern branch in a south easterly direction. The point of the likely second reversal has been obscured by earthworks connected with a later water course, but, further to the west, nearer the quarry, there are more earthworks which could well be connected with the trackbed of the probable line running to the top of the quarry.

Make your way back down the road until you come to the wooden hut on the north side of the road (point 7).

(The return route outlined below is over rough moor and can be very wet underfoot at times. If this is not to your liking, return the way you came as far as the water authority houses just east of the south end of Lower Gorple Reservoir. Here turn right onto the Pennine Way and follow it up the hill as far as the quarry on the hillside. Here you can pick up the walk again at point 12.)

Opposite the wooden hut in the clough below you will see a wooden board acting as a footbridge over the stream. Note also the position of a stone house about a third of a mile to the south east. Cross over the wooden board and make your way along the path which hugs the east side of the stream at the bottom of the tributary clough leading off to the south.

Follow the clough until its widens out and an old stone wall comes down to it from the south east. Leave the clough here and follow this wall, keeping it on your right. Soon the ruins of Raistrick Greave, the house you noted farther back, comes into sight again. The right of way passes immediately to the east of the house in a rush filled lane.

[9] Just past the ruins the path emerges onto open moor. At the point where the old stone wall on your left makes a right-angled bend away to the north east, bear slightly left and then continue straight on to the south east. The path as used now is only faintly visible and runs just to the left of a slight hollow over the moor which marks the remains of an old way leading passed Raistrick to Heptonstall. As the path levels off, after a steady pull uphill, some lengths of a single line of stone slabs laid for the old way become visible. Over on your left you now have a good overall view of Lower Gorple Reservoir in its lonely moorland setting.

[10] Soon after the path levels off a path branches off to the south to cross over the brow of the hill. Don't be misled into following this! Instead keep on the path which continues along the contour to the east south east until you come to the remains of Reaps Cross (a stone wall is not far away from it to the south east). Part of the shaft of the cross still stands, while the top half lies nearby on the ground.

[11] From the cross strike north eastwards over the flat area of ground until you reach an unmetalled road crossing the neck from south to north. Follow this as it leads north down hill towards Lower Gorple Reservoir.

[12] After just under a quarter of a mile you will find yourself level with one of the quarries opened up to provide stone for the reservoir works. A map in H. Bowtell's 'Reservoirs Railways of the Yorkshire Pennines' shows what is listed as a 'loco worked incline' leading up to these quarries. How this branch linked up to the quarry is not, however, clear on the ground.

On your right was the puddle field, which has left its mark on the hillside. Just below the puddle field you can easily spot a concrete structure which, presumably, had something to do with the puddle field, though it is not at the top of the incline as one might expect if it was connected with the latter.

This double tracked incline serving the puddle field crossed over the road you are on about a 100 yards below the quarry and a little above the a wooden gate over the road. The trackbed of the incline is only slightly raised but can easily be made out.

[13] Go through the gate and continue along the rough road until you reach the concrete surfaced road belonging to the Yorkshire Water Authority. The easiest way back from here to the start of the walk is to turn right onto this concrete road and follow it as it runs eastwards above Graining Water until you reach the public road where the walk began.

Walk 3: The Brownhill Reservoir Railway

Map: Pathfinder Map 714 SE 00/10

Distance: approximately 5 miles

Start: The picnic car park on the north side of Digley Reservoir, $3/4$ mile west of Holmfirth of 'Summer Wine' fame. Grid reference SE 110 072.

By Car: The picnic car park is situated to the north of the A6024 Woodhead to Holmfirth road. It is signposted both at Holmbridge and Holme 1 $1/2$ and 2 $1/2$ miles respectively south west of Holmfirth. (There is also a picnic car park above the east side of Ramsden Reservoir for those who wish to do only the 'railway part' of the walk).

By Public Transport: There is a regular bus service from Huddersfield to Holmbridge through which the walk passes.

A pleasant ramble which gives some fine views of the eastern slopes of the Pennines below Holme Moss as well as exploring the considerable remains of a fairly short but interesting narrow gauge reservoir railway. The walk begins well away from the Brownhill Reservoir as the writer feels it is always better, if possible, to explore a railway from its beginning to its end rather than start in the middle. The going underfoot is quite easy except for one section on rough pasture which can be quite wet at times.

The Railway

The main contract for Brownhill Reservoir was let in 1924 to Lehane, Mackenzie, Shand & Co. Ltd. of Darely Dale. This reservoir was the last of four built for the Corporation of the West Riding town of Batley. The other three reservoirs, all of which will be passed on the walk, were Riding Wood, Yateholm (both completed about 1878) and Ramsden (completed in 1883 but not in use until 1892).

Preliminary work on Brownhill Reservoir began in August 1924 but the official inauguration ceremony did not take place until 18 May 1925. To service the construction work a three-foot gauge railway system was laid down, the main line of which ran from the depot at the northern end of the future retaining wall to the site of the puddle clay field about a mile away to the south, high up on the hillside just on the thousand foot contour. As the depot was at about 750 feet above sea level, this involved a climb of 250 feet. Branching off the 'main line' about a third of a mile from the depot was a short branch leading to principal quarry served by the system. Immediately after this junction was the main engineering feature of the system, namely, a spectacular trestle bridge reminiscent of those built in the pioneering days of the railways in the west of the United States. After crossing this bridge the railway began a 1 in 20 climb up the side of the hill to the puddle field.

Eight 0-4-0 steam locomotives (two well tank and six saddle tank) are known to have worked on this system. They came from a variety of makers which included the German firm of Orenstein & Keppel. The site offices, workshops and locomotive sheds were situated in what is now a wood immediately to the east of the northern end of the retaining wall. There was no rail connection to the nearest standard gauge railhead at Holmfirth so castings, valves, filter houses machinery, etc., as well as the engines themselves had to be brought from the station there by road.

Looking southwards as the retaining wall of Brownhill Reservoir nears completion. View from the valley side opposite to point 3 on the walk. *Reproduced by kind permission from The Harold Bowtell Collection.*

By 1930 all the major work had been completed so the railway would have been dismantled sometime between then and 24 May 1932 when the reservoir was formally opened.

The Walk

[1] On leaving the car park take the road leading downhill in a southerly direction. When you come to the north end of the reservoir retaining wall, take the road that goes off to the left in the direction of Holmbridge. On your right you soon pass a stone shed. Just after this, where the wire fence ends and the stone wall begins, is a kissing gate. Go through, turn left and for a few paces proceed along, keeping immediately to the right of the stone wall. The path next drops down the slope at an oblique angle leading to some steps which finish at a hard surfaced road. Go left here and follow the road as it takes you along a delightful little valley leading down to Holmbridge.

[2] At Holmbridge turn right onto the main road (A6024) and make your way to the south, with the parish church on you left. Leave the main road where it bends to the right, keeping straight on instead, following the road signposted 'Yateholm'. After the mill and stone house on the right the road turns to the right and climbs gently up the valley to bring one level with the southern end of the retaining wall of Brownhill Reservoir.

[3] The reservoir railway zigzagged around at several points where the wall is now. On the far side you can see some woods growing on the site of the engine sheds and the depot. A public path goes across the wall if you wish to search for traces on the other side. There is some evidence of ground disturbance on the opposite side of the road at the southern end of the retaining wall though the map in Harold Bowtell's book on the railway does not show any track at this point.

Continue along the road as it curves gently round to the south. On your right you now have a good view of the reservoir. The main line of the reservoir railway ran on the opposite side on the eastern side of the by-wash channel. The by-wash channel below you also once carried some railway tracks. Continue on along the road.

[4] As you proceed a spur of the reservoir filling the valley of Rake Dike comes into view. A short branch led off from the main line on the northern side of the spur to a stone quarry which you can see from where you are standing. The Rake Dike itself was crossed by an impressive trestle bridge mentioned earlier. After this bridge the railway began its steep climb up to the puddle field. This section can be clearly

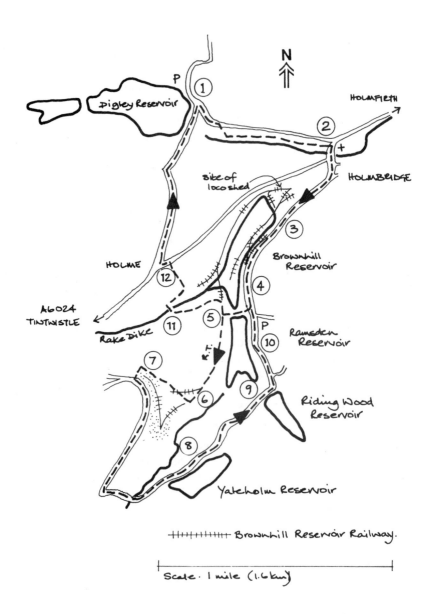

N

P

Digley Reservoir
①

②
HOLMFIRTH

+
HOLMBRIDGE

Site of
loco shed

③
Brownhill
Reservoir

HOLME

④

⑫

A6024
TINTWISTLE

⑪
⑤
P
⑩
Ramsden
Reservoir

Rake Dike

R.T.

⑦

⑥
⑨

Riding Wood
Reservoir

⑧

Yateholm Reservoir

┼┼┼┼┼┼┼┼┼┼┼ Brownhill Reservoir Railway.

Scale. 1 mile (1.6 km)

Brownhill Reservoir viewed from the trackbed of the reservoir railway as it climbs up the hillside towards the puddle field.

seen as a terrace running first through the oak wood and then, having passed the top of the western end of the wall of Ramsden Reservoir, up along the open valley slope.

Continue on along the road until, just after crossing a cattle grid (note the use of electric tram rails), a path leads down on the right to cross over the valley on the bank of the Ramsden Reservoir. Go along this path to the west side of the reservoir.

The crossing of this path by the railway at the west end of the reservoir bank has been obscured but a stone revetted terrace is visible just south of the former crossing point.

[5] Follow the path as it bends round to the right. Just after passing two iron bollards the trackbed going down to the right of the path can be clearly seen. Very soon a high wooden stile appears on your left. Cross over this and go left following the path signposted 'Yateholm'. This is a permissive path made by the Yorkshire Water Authority. Follow the path as it climbs a little to cross an old stone wall and then drops down to a good stone wall bounding the reservoir.

At this point the path joins the trackbed of the Brownhill Reservoir Railway and makes a pleasant walk as it climbs steadily up the side of the valley. Those with a little bit of imagination can produce visions of the little four-wheeled steam locomotives puffing and snorting their way up the bank pulling their trains of 'empties' up to the puddle field beyond. The trackbed is mostly terraced out from the hillside but there is a short section of embankment across a little depression in the hillside. As the trackbed reaches the lip of the lower part of the valley and the ground begins to flatten out the course of the railway begins to turn to the right. Here the path leaves the trackbed and drops down the slope to the left.

[6] Just before the footbridge in the clough below is reached you come to a three-way footpath signpost. Turn sharp right up the bank following the footpath signposted 'Holme' (at the time of writing the 'Holme' sign was lying on the ground but pointing in the right direction). After a steep but short climb up the slope the path levels out.

Just after the point on your left where a corner of stone wall juts out and a wire fence begins, the railway once crossed over the path. The trackbed can be faintly discerned on your right, while on your left an embankment is clear enough. Cross over the rather wet area and continue on along the path as it climbs steadily uphill to the west just to the left of a tumbled stone wall.

After a few paces if you look back you will see that the railway trackbed on the north east side of the path can now be more clearly made out. Careful observers may also be able to make out the course of a branch leading off to the west. This branch crosses the path further on.

The main line of the railway reached the puddle field via a reversal in a field away to the south west. This is not particularly obvious from where you are now but it will become more obvious further on the walk. The puddle clay field itself stretched in a long thick band along the south west side of the path right up to the brow of the slope. The disturbed nature of the ground here remains to remind us of it.

[7] Continue on along the path until you reach the brow of the slope and then make for the large wooden stile over the fence a little uphill to your left, just to the right of a big sycamore tree.

As you make for the stile, note that the disturbed ground ends just a little to the west. Presumably this marks the end of the puddle field and therefore of the railway.

Cross the stile and go left on the hard surfaced but unmetalled road you find yourself on.

As the road bends round to the south, you should be able to spot the trackbed of the Brownhill Reservoir Railway as it came up to the reversal neck and then bent round to the north west on its final climb up to the top end of the puddle field.

Looking northwards between points 5 and 11 on the walk this view shows how the reservoir railway crossed the Holme Valley on an impressive trestle bridge. Four wagons on the left stand on the branch to the quarry. *Reproduced by kind permission from The Harold Bowtell Collection.*

Continue on now along the road which after going southwards turns to the east, passed Yateholm Reservoir (built 1872/78) and Riding Wood Reservoir (also built 1872/78) and then turns to the north to bring you back to eastern end of the retaining wall of Ramsden Reservoir. The road needs no description to follow (ignore all tracks leading off to the right and the footpath going off to the left) but you may find it worth while making three observation stops on the way.

[8] The first stop suggested is opposite the middle of the retaining wall of Yateholm Reservoir (a tall grass bank on your right) immediately before the start of the second fir tree plantation on the north side of the road. Look back towards the site of the puddle field and, with binoculars at least, you should be able to make out clearly the course the railway on its final climb to the top of the puddle field after leaving the reversal neck.

[9] The second suggested stop is on the road as it crosses over the retaining wall of Riding Wood Reservoir. Here, on the left, at the bottom of the wall, you will see a stone quarry. Which reservoir construction project this quarry was opened out for one cannot be certain but if it was for the Ramsden Reservoir then there must have been some sort of tramroad leading north from here to the site of the retaining wall. You will also notice a well embanked trackway leading north from this quarry. This may well have carried the tramway, though, on the other hand, it may have been made simply to cover some water piping.

[10] The last suggested stop comes when you are on the road on the east side of the Ramsden Reservoir. From here you will get a good overall view of the upper section of the Brownhill Reservoir Railway trackbed as it climbs up the west side of the valley to the puddle field.

When you get back to the retaining wall of the Ramsden Reservoir cross over on the footpath to the west side once again. This time, however, once on the other side ignore the large wooden stile on your left. Instead keep straight on to the north, following the well used path to the village of Holme.

As the path bends round to the west you will be able to note below you to the north the site of the former trestle viaduct over the Rake Dike. Unfortunately, trees now somewhat obscure the view but the quarry with the course of its short branch line on the north side of Rake Dike can be more easily seen.

The path up to Holme Village is well used and easy to follow with no diverging paths or trackways so there is no need for a detailed description.

[11] The path drops down to a footbridge over Rake Dike and then, almost reversing direction, climbs up the other side. At the top it bends left to reach the main road at the north west end of Holme.

[12] Here turn left and then go down the first road on your right (signpost to Digley Reservoir picnic car park) which will bring you back to the start of the walk. Those using public transport can shorten the walk if they wish by catching a bus from Holme.

Walk 4: The Chew Reservoir Railway

Map: Pathfinder Map 714 SE 00/10

Distance: about 5 $1/2$ miles.

Start: Dove Stone picnic car park situated below the retaining wall of Dove Stone Reservoir about 1 mile east of Greenfield. Grid reference SE 013 035.

By Car: The lane to the car park, (Bank Lane), leads southwards off the A635 Holmfirth to Mossley road, about $3/8$ of a mile east of the junction with the A669 (Chew Valley Road) at the east end of Greenfield. Bank Lane leading to the car park is the only road off to the south at this point but can easily be missed as the sign post to Dove Stone Reservoir is neither very conspicuous or well sited.

By Public Transport: From Greenfield Station on the Manchester to Huddersfield line the walk can be joined by going east along Chew Valley Road (A669) to its junction with the Holmfirth to Mossley road (A635) by the Clarence Hotel. (Bus routes 352 and 355 run as far this point.) From here the walk is best joined at point [2] by taking the path up the hillside to the south. Directions can be found on p. 48

This walk explores the eastern half of a reservoir railway climbing right up to the top of the moors at the head of the spectacular Chew Valley on the eastern side of the southern Pennines. There is on the walk a very steep climb which can, however, be by-passed. The last part of the walk is on peat moor and may be very wet underfoot. The rest is easy going.

The Railway

In 1905 the Ashway Gap Estate was bought by the Ashton, Stalybridge & Dukinfield Waterworks Committee for £12,000 with a view to the construction of a reservoir high up on the moors at the head of Chew Brook at 1,600 feet above sea-level. On completion, the reservoir was at the time the highest in the British Isles. Work was slow in getting under way and in 1907 the waterworks committee applied for a bill to allow an extension of ten years for the completion of the reservoir. The main contractors were Morrison and Mason.

In 1908 work on the reservoir is described as being in full swing. In order to service this remote construction site a three-foot gauge railway was laid down from the London and North Western Railway at Micklehurst near Mossley to the site of the reservoir four miles away and 1,100 feet higher. In order to help overcome the difference in height between the two ends of the line an incline, with the steep gradient of 1 in 4, was constructed half a mile west of the construction site on the steep slope below Dish Stone Rocks. The incline was worked by a steam winch. One engine known to have worked on the line was a Bagnall made 0-4-0 saddle tank called 'The Preston', which was built in 1908 for use on Preston Corporation's reservoir construction site at Longridge. It was next used by Morrison and Mason in the Chew Valley.

Beside the normal construction traffic there was a 'Paddy Mail' which brought construction site workers from Micklehurst as far as the foot of the incline. In 1908, while working on the excavation of the trench at the site of the reservoir retaining wall, two men were seriously injured in an accident caused by blast misfiring. One poor man had his face half blown off while the other was struck on the head. They both had to be carried down the mountainside and put on the 'Paddy Mail' at the foot of the incline from where they were taken to Micklehurst. Later one of them died from his injuries.

There is an instance in 1911 of the public being carried on the railway, at least by special arrangement, when the Saddleworth Literary & Philosophical Society travelled on the line in order to visit the 'new waterworks at Chew Wells'. In 1913 the reservoir was filled with water but more work needed to be done because of leakage. The railway was presumably dismantled soon afterwards.

The eastern half of this remarkable reservoir railway's course, the part which the walk will explore, is well-preserved and easily traceable. The course of the western half, on the other hand, has been almost completely obliterated, presumably because of reinstatement where it crossed agricultural land. Perhaps the best way to spot the few traces of the course of the railway as it winds round the hillside above Greenfield is to go high up on the north east side of the valley above Grasscroft (for example, at Grid ref. SD 978 049) on a clear winter's day and look back across the valley with a pair of binoculars. The last part of the course of the railway towards Micklehurst seems to have left no clear trace at all.

The Walk

[1] From the car park make your way west along the lane that bears off to the west immediately to the south of the stone information and toilet block building. After a quarter of a mile some terraced houses are passed on the right. The lane then becomes stone bottomed and starts to gently climb up the side of the Chew Valley. About another quarter of a mile further on, the course of the Chew Reservoir Railway can be made out on the hillside to your left, a little above the lane you are on.

[2] As the lane bends left on the final part of the climb up to the hamlet of Fern Lee, it is crossed by the course of the railway. A few yards to the west of the crossing, however, the trackbed of the railway has been destroyed where it continued to the west north west of the northern-most house of the hamlet. There is, however, more to be seen of the course of the railway further to the west.

Make your way through the hamlet of Fern Lee and continue along the lane that runs to the west for about 200 yards until you come to the start of the third field west of the hamlet on your right.

[3] Here (by the gap stile) look to the north down the field, and halfway between where you are standing and the little reservoir near the bottom of the field, you can make out the course of the railway as it continues to the west, running on a low embankment. Further west of here, as there are only slight traces of the course of railway remaining, the walk reverses direction to go east to trace the remains of this remarkable reservoir railway as it makes its way up to the moors above the head of the Chew Valley.

Make your way back to the hamlet. Passing through the hamlet, keep right and take the trackway that leads off to the east (branching off from the lane you came up along) by the southernmost house in the hamlet. Continue along the trackway as it bends to the south east, ignoring any stiles or gates on your left. Below you, on your left, the trackbed of the railway is easily made out as it runs along, terraced out from the hillside with a few small short embankments, until it disappears into a conifer plantation.

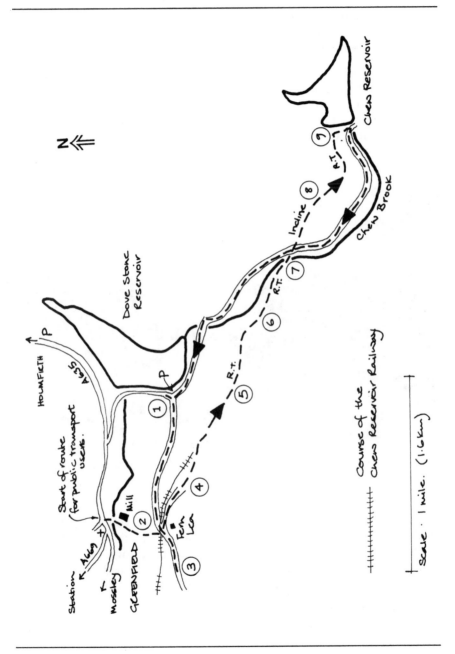

[4] Further on the trackway becomes a mere footpath and enters the plantation at a kissing gate. Here a glance down the ride or opening in the trees on your left will reveal a short section of the railway trackbed.

Follow the path as it goes eastwards between two fences in the plantation until you come to an open space in the trees. Here the path drops down a little and then joins the course of the railway trackbed which can be seen emerging from the plantation on the left. From now on you are able to walk on the course of the railway until it ends at Chew Reservoir.

A view of the course of the Chew Reservoir tramway as it winds its way up to the base of the incline.

[5] Further on the trees and a kissing gate allow you to follow the trackbed of the railway as it runs across a pasture field. The railway crossed a small stream here, either on a trestle bridge or on a now destroyed embankment. Beyond, however, the trackbed is clear and easy to follow as it continues to the east, still climbing gently.

Immediately beyond the next kissing gate the railway crossed another stream on a trestle bridge. The remains of the timber baulks of this trestle bridge can be seen poking out of the tracked in the east side. At the next stream the water has cut into the trackbed, enabling you to see that the upper surface of the trackbed was laid with clinker.

After passing by a massive boulder you come to another kissing gate which gives access to a wood through which the trackbed of the railway is especially well preserved. Above, on the right, an impressive outcrop of rocks called Wimberry Stones towers above.

[6] Leaving the wood, the course of the railway passes through a little cutting which is stone revetted on the right side. This is the first of several examples of stone revetting of cuttings and embankments which is quite remarkable on a railway that, even at the time of its construction, was known to have a limited life.

A stile follows and beyond that a deep gully, no doubt, crossed by a trestle bridge, the abutments of which remain on the north west side. An impressive section of narrow gauge railway engineering follows as the course of the railway winds round the hillside through a mass of tumbled boulders on revetted sided embankments or terraces. Ahead the incline, which carried the railway 500 feet up out of the valley, can be seen leading up the hillside. Strangely, its course is more easily made out from a distance than nearby.

[7] An especially well revetted and high stone terrace brings the railway trackbed to the crossing of the Chew Brook. The railway bridge, presumably wooden, has gone but its well made stone abutments remain. There is a modern wooden footbridge below the trackbed to take you across the brook.

Once over the brook follow the course of the railway as it bends round to the right to a large flat area where the wagons were marshalled before going up or after coming down the steeply graded (1 in 4) incline up the hillside to the east. If you go to the end of the flat section and look back at the bottom of the incline you will see that it too has a good revetted stone side to the south.

Make your way up the incline trackbed to where it crosses the metalled road running up to the reservoir. The suggested route continues up the course of the incline but those who feel that the climb is too steep can make their way to the right along the road to the north end of the reservoir retaining wall (point 9) from where they can follow the course of the railway back to the top of the incline. The suggested route from here onwards is on open access land which may be closed off to the public on certain days during the grouse shooting season.

Above the road, at first, there appears to be no sign of the incline but a scramble up by the little watercourse will soon reveal its course again as it climbs steeply upwards through two shallow cuttings. The primary surface of the incline has been eroded away but the underneath stone work is clear enough. After the second cutting the incline levels out a little, at least comparatively speaking, and widens a little to enable wagons going up and down to pass. The width of the formation seems to suggest that it was of the three-rail with passing loop type.

[8] Another steep climb and a few more puffs bring you to the top of the incline on the edge of the peat moor near Dish Stone Rocks. There was a steam winch at the top of the incline to haul the loaded wagons up but its site is not clear.

To take the railway to the site of reservoir retaining wall a cutting was made through the peat. This has now been partly filled in but enough of the original excavation is left to enable you to follow the course of the railway without any difficulty as it goes off to the south east from the incline top. Next it bends round to the north east to reach what is now the middle half of the Chew Reservoir retaining wall.

[9] At the construction site, where the retaining wall now rises, there must have been several sidings and short branches but of these nothing remains except perhaps the trackbed of a possible branch leading away from the top of the south end of the reservoir wall to what appears to be some sort of a dump on the hillside, a little to the west.

To make your way back descend down to the bottom of the retaining wall and pick up the metalled road which will take you back to the car park where the walk started.

Suggested Connecting Route for Public Transport Users

A 100 yards passed the Clarence Hotel at the junction of the A635 and the A669 roads take the metalled road that leads off to the south east, crossing the Chew Brook by cement bridge and then going southwards to the west of Waterside Mill. At the south west end of the mill follow the lane as it goes round the west side of the second row of terraced houses.

Where the lane turns to the south round the southern end of the terraced houses go over the stile on your right. Follow the path as it goes uphill, keeping to the left of a metal fence and then a stone wall. Just before an old quarry is reached, about halfway up the hill, cross over the wooden stile on your right and then continue uphill, keeping to the right of a low, collapsed stone wall, aiming for the houses of Fern Lee hamlet ahead. At the top of the field go through the gateway (the reservoir railway crossed just below this) and make your way up to the stile which gives you access to the lane linking the hamlet with Dove Stone Reservoir car park to the east. You are here at point [2] on the walk.

On your return walk a good path can be found running down to the point where you started immediately west of the terraced house on the lane leading west from Dove Stone Reservoir on the south side of the valley.

Walk 5: The Peak Forest Tramway: Buxworth to Chapel-en-le-Frith

Map: Pathfinder Map 742 SK 08/18 or Outdoor Leisure Map 1 'The Peak District Dark Peak Area'.

Distance: 6 miles

Start: The canal basin at Buxworth in the Goyt Valley. Grid reference SK 023 821.

By Car: The turning to Buxworth is on the north side of the A6, Stockport to Buxton road just over half a mile south of Furness Vale and about $^3/_4$ of a miles north west of the round-about at the west end of the Whaley Bridge Chapel-en-le-Frith by-pass. The turning is immediately east of the railway bridge and involves a sharp left turn when approaching from the Stockport direction. In Buxworth you turn sharp right at the T junction to reach the canal basin just a few yards further on.

By Public Transport: There is a regular train service to Whaley Bridge from where Buxworth canal basin can be reached by a walk of about one mile along the canal tow-path.

This walk is the first of two exploring an interesting and remarkable early railway which ran through the attractive hills of north west Derbyshire. The going underfoot is not too difficult, though boots are advised. Some climbing but nothing too strenuous.

The Railway

The origin of this line goes back to 1793 when some of the backers of an abortive scheme to link the Cromford and Ashton Canals via the Wye Valley gave their support to a less ambitious scheme to link the limestone quarries in the Buxton area to the Ashton Canal. This scheme proposed that the link should consist of a canal to Chapel Milton from where a plate-way type railway would lead to the quarries at Loads Knowle. To further the scheme the Peak Forest Canal Company was formed on 28 March 1794. The Act of the following year, authorising the canal part of the scheme, also sanctioned a 'communication by Railways or Stone Roads' from Bugsworth (now Buxworth) to Loads Knowle near Dove Holes. The reason for Bugsworth and not Chapel Milton being the canal end of the plate-way was that the surveyor and builder of the line, Benjamin Outram, considered that the gradient of the Bugsworth - Chapel Milton section of the proposed canal line would involve too many locks and that, therefore, this part would be more economically served by running the plate-way to Bugsworth.

The plate-way or tramway was completed somewhere around 1799 as a single line. In 1803 most of the line was doubled. The tramway was laid to the gauge of four feet two-and-a-half inches, using an 'L' section rail. Each rail was three feet in length and laid on stone slabs in which holes were drilled. The rail was held in place by means of an iron slipper or chair which was fixed to the stone slabs by means of an oak wood peg. The original rails were cast iron but these were later replaced by steel rails of longer length. At level crossings a 'U'-shaped rail was used. As horses were the sole motive power for the line, a cobbled path was laid between the rails.

The early wagons on the Peak Forest Tramway looked little different from farm carts except that they had smaller wooden wheels which were shod with iron. Later wagons looked more railway like and had cast iron wheels. Being a plate-way the wheels were, of course, flangeless. Rail friction was reduced, or at least the operators hoped it would be, by the use of a drip can placed over the leading wheels. The braking system was primitive to say the least. The brakes man would leap from the moving wagon and thrust iron sprags into the spokes of the spinning wheels which would then lock and, hopefully, bring the train of wagons to a halt. An alternative method was to use two large hooks with three links of chain between to bring the moving wheel to a halt. It is hardly surprising that several men lost their arms while trying to bring their wagons to a stop.

The carriage of limestone was the life blood of the tramway. There were, however, sidings to the mills adjoining the line and there is evidence of some agricultural traffic. The six mile line was divided into three sections, the short middle one of which consisted of a self-acting incline linking the two outer longer sections worked by horse and gravity. The first section from Buxsworth rose 206 feet in three miles on an average gradient of 1 in 80 to the bottom of the incline at Chapel-en-le-Frith. It is this section that the first walk will cover.

Teams of five horses were used to haul the empty wagons up from the canal basin at Buxworth to the foot of the incline. The journey with the loaded wagons from the foot of the incline down to the canal basin was made by gravity with the wagons linked into trains or 'gangs' of as many as 40 at a time, accompanied by the brakes man riding on the axle pin of the leading wagon. The Buxworth canal basin must have been a hive of activity at the height of the tramway's operation with stone being discharged from the wagons either directly into the canal barges below or into storage bays or into the several kilns situated on both sides of the basin. There was a special 'wheel' by means of which the contents of each wagon in turn was tipped directly via a hinged end plate into the boat below. Cranes as well as manpower helped to unload the boats.

The Peak Forest Tramway eventually came into the ownership of the Great Central Railway and, after grouping, into that of the London and North Eastern Railway. It had a remarkably long life, over a century in fact. This was especially notable in view of the fact that the tramway's method of working was virtually the same at the time of its closure as it was at the time of its opening. In the early years of our century traffic faded away and by 1926 the tramway was completely out of use. The rails were lifted but the square stone sleepers were largely left in situ. Today, despite much damage to the course of the line, there is still much to be seen over the whole length of the former tramway.

The Walk

[1] After you have finished examining the fascinating Buxworth canal basin take the trackway that leads away to the east between the river on the north and the new A6 road on the south. The trackway is on the trackbed of the Peak Forest Tramway.

Soon a bridge with associated embankments appears on the north side of the trackway. These are the remains of a branch line which diverted away from the 'main line' to pass over the road from Buxworth to the canal basin at a higher level than the rest of the system in order to reach some lime kilns situated to the north of the canal basin. The south side of the embankment on your side of the river has been damaged but a glance from its eastern end will reveal the north side with its perpendicular stone reinforcement still intact. Near the junction with the main line a few stone sleepers can be seen.

The Canal Basin at Bugsworth (now Buxworth) with loaded wagons to be moved the final few yards for their loads of stone to be transhipped into canal barges. *Reproduced by kind permission from The D. Ripley Collection.*

Just beyond the stone houses on the right a branch line led off to the south to lower part of Crist Quarries but of this nothing remains to be seen from this point.

Continue along the trackway which continues to follow the course of the tramway as it runs between the river and the new A6 road. The section with new stone walls bordering the trackway marks a slight diversion to accommodate the new road. Whatever one feels about this new road, at least we can be thankful that direct damage to the remain of this historic tramway was limited to this.

[2] After a straight run, the trackway on the tramway trackbed bends right and then left, past Whitehall Works where there was once a tramway siding.

[3] After passing the millpond on the north side, the road to Whitehough is crossed. Here the tramway trackbed becomes a pleasant greenway as it bends round close to the Black Brook and then bends

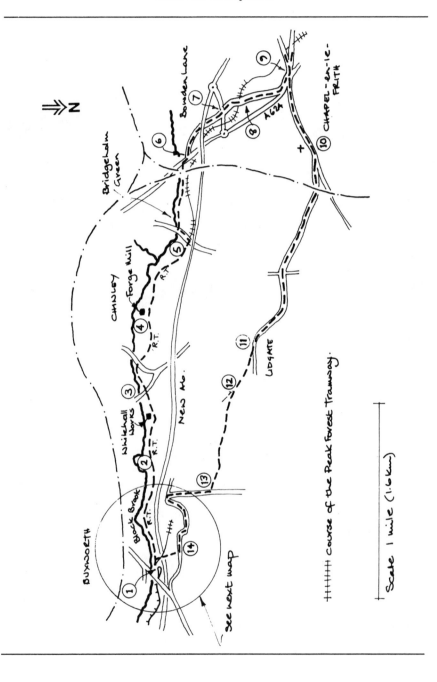

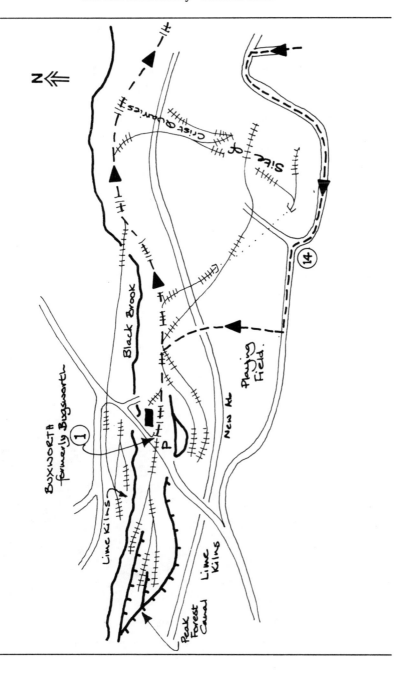

right to cross the Chinley to Whitehough road on the level. East of the crossing the trackbed becomes a trackway once more. Proceed on.

[4] As you draw level with some modern factory buildings on your left, the first of several sets of stone sleepers appear. After passing Forge Mill (there was a siding here also) and its dam, the trackway bends to the right. Here again many stone sleepers remain in place and visible. Unfortunately, once you get level with the sewage works on your left you will find that the trackbed has been covered with cement.

[5] Soon the trackway, or cement way as it has become, ends at the road to Bridgeholm Green. From here onwards there is no right of way on the course of the tramway which, for the first section beyond here, has been covered with tarmac to make a private road. Your exploration, therefore, of the Peak Forest Tramway must now continue on footpaths and lanes which run roughly parallel to the course of the tramway.

Turn left on the road and follow it as it goes north eastwards until you come to a stone bridge over the Black Brook with a large stone mill on the other side. Don't cross over the bridge but go through the gap stile

The trackway near point 4 still has many of the stone sleepers in place.

in the wall on your right and then make your way eastwards between some outer buildings of the mill on the south side of the brook.

Beyond the mill grounds the path is easy to follow as it goes through two gap stiles (both next to gates), keeping to the south of the brook. The course of the tramway can be seen running on the other side of the stone wall with a high wire fence immediately behind it. Cross over the wooden stile under the railway viaduct, keep straight on and cross the bridge ahead to gain the main Glossop to Chapel-en-le-Frith road.

A glance to the south will reveal some outer buildings of the Ferodo Company. These stand on the course of the tramway at approximately the point where it entered the only tunnel on the line. The tunnel took the tramway under what is now the main road. Of the tunnel's western portal nothing is to be seen now, but, as you will see further on on the walk, its eastern portal is intact.

[6] Cross the main road and proceed along it to the south east. After a few paces, go left off the road and proceed along Bowden Lane which branches off to the left. Follow the lane as it goes under the new A6 road viaduct until you come to a ruined building on your right looking like a little folly type castle. Take the path that runs from the south side of this building to new link road from the A624 road to the new A6 road.

[7] Once on the link road, turn right and make your way to the middle of the bridge carrying the link road over the river. Here look to the north west. On the other side of the river you will see the embankment of the tramway leading up to the river (its bridge has gone) with the eastern portal of the tunnel visible in winter, at least.

Go back to the stile by which you gained access to the link road. Cross over the road and go over the stile opposite (on the south side). Turn right and go through the gap stile in the wall in front of you. This gives access to the tramway trackbed which can be observed bearing away to the south east to the left of the works car park. There is no right of way here along the course of the tramway so it is necessary to return to the link road. Back on the road make your way eastwards until the crossing with Bowden Lane is reached. Here turn right and go south down the lane.

A few paces down the lane, where it bends to the right, the tramway crossed over on the level. A white gate and some old garages on the east side of the road, just to the left of the private road going down to the works ahead, mark the point of the crossing.

[8] Continue along the lane. Just past the works on your left you will see a footpath (signposted) leading off to the north east. A diversion along this footpath will bring you once more to the course of the tramway which is clearly to be seen running between its original boundary walls. At the time of writing a number of stone sleepers had been piled up against the boundary wall immediately north of the path where it crosses over the trackbed. Make your way back to the lane and continue on into Chapel-en-le-Frith.

[9] Keep going left until you reach the main road to Buxton. Going east on this road, after about 75 yards, you will come to a fork. Take the left fork (signposted 'Buxton ... Edale'). A few paces further on you will come to the point where the tramway crossed over the road. This was immediately east of the stone bridge. Be careful not to miss as it is

This more detailed view of the inclined plane at Chapel-en-le-Frith shows clearly the disc signal, the flanged rails and the wire rope on the incline. The two boys in their Sunday best show that this is not a working day. *Reproduced by kind permission from The D. Ripley Collection.*

Taken from near point 8 on the walk this view of the incline plane at Chapel-en-le-Frith captures the essence of the High Peak Tramway. *Reproduced by kind permission from The D. Ripley Collection.*

visible as a bridge only on the north side of the road. The council road depot opposite is, in fact, situated on the sidings at the bottom of the only incline plane on the tramway. Unfortunately, not much remains of the tramway here, so retrace your steps back to the road junction. Turn sharp left here and go east along the former Buxton road for a few yards until you find yourself above the road depot.

A look over the wall on your left will reveal (between the asbestos roofed building and a stone house) the now filled in bridge which took the tramway under the road. Cross over the road and on the other side you will have a good view of the incline, called locally 'The Plane', going up the hillside. Many a young local would no doubt have stood here in years gone by, watching the wagons clattering and creaking as they were wound up and down the incline. You can imagine the din as sometimes the wire or chain would break and the wagons would come rushing down hill at breakneck speed to pile up under the bridge. It could even have been dangerous to have stood where you are now. It is recorded that on one occasion during the First World War one break away wagon even flew over the bridge to land in the yard on the other side!

This is as far as this walk takes you in the exploration of the remains of the Peak Forest Tramway. The next walk will explore the upper section of the incline and the line beyond. The introduction to this walk will give further information about the incline.

The suggested return route makes for Buxworth approximately as the crow flies. It does, unfortunately, involve quite a lot of tarmac road walking but does give some good views.

[10] Make your way to the centre of Chapel-en-le-Frith along the main road until you reach the Market Place on your right. Here make for the north west corner and pick up Eccles Road. Follow Eccles Road eastwards. On your way you pass under the former main line of the Midland Railway and soon open country appears on your right.

[11] Continue along Eccles Road over the road junction at Higher Crossing and up the hill until you get just past Lidgate Farm (farmhouse on your left and farm building on your right) where the Black Brook Valley comes into view. Go over the stile (next to a gate) on the north side of the road. Turn left and follow the clear grass trackway which runs along the contour to the west. The trackway is so well terraced out on the hillside that it once must have been a good cart road.

[12] After just over 300 yards you reach a fork in the green trackway. Take the left-hand fork which keeps to the west and climbs very slightly upwards. As you proceed, on your right you should have a fine view of the Black Brook Valley with the course of the Peak Forest Tramway winding below and the ex-Midland Railway line of British Rail on the other side. After about another 300 yards the green trackway becomes enclosed between stone walls and becomes a green lane.

[13] A quarter of a mile further on the green lane makes a T-junction with a narrow tarmac lane running south-north. Turn right and follow this lane northwards. A look to the north west will reveal to the observant eye, just over a quarter of a mile away, the trackbed of the Peak Forest Tramway's branch leading to the upper part of Crist Quarries (now filled in). The clearest section of the branch is where it ran on an embankment immediately south of the new A6 road.

After a quarter of a mile the lane you are on makes a T-junction with another lane. Go left here and follow this lane as it bends past the vast pile of in-fill that marks the site of Crist Quarries.

[14] Where the lane turns to the left at the first houses of Barren Clough a short diversion down the lane branching off to the right will bring you to the remains of the branch to the upper part of Crist Quarries mentioned above.

About 150 yards west along the road from the start of the houses of Barren Clough a footpath on your right running down the east side of a football field will take you back to the start of the walk at Buxworth.

Walk 6: The Peak Forest Tramway : Chapel-en-le-Frith to Dove Holes

Map: Pathfinder Maps 742 SK 08/18 and 760 SK 07/17 or Outdoor Leisure Maps 1 'The Peak District Dark Peak Area' and 24 'The Peak District White Peak Area'.

Distance: 4 miles.

Start: The market place in the middle of Chapel-en-le-Frith. Grid reference SK 057 807.

By Car: The exits to Chapel-en-le-Frith are well signposted towards the eastern end of the Whaley Bridge to Chapel-en-le-Frith by-pass on the A6 Stockport to Buxton road. In the town there is a large car park just south east of the Market Place on the south side of the main road. There is also a car park by the entrance to the former Midland Railway station north west of the Market Place.

By Public Transport: There is a regular train service to Chapel-en-le-Frith on the Stockport to Buxton line. The station is a little out of the town but the return section of the walk passes the station.

This walk explores the upper part of the Peak Forest Tramway. Mainly on footpaths with some interesting changes of scenery.

The Railway

The general outline of the story of the Peak Forest Tramway is dealt with in the introduction to the previous walk.

The upper section of the tramway, which this walk will explore, started from the top of 'The Plane' or the incline above Chapel-en-le-Frith. The incline itself was 512 yards long and rose 209 feet. As the loads of stone going downhill far exceeded in weight any loads needing to go uphill the incline was of the self-acting type. At the top was a wooden tower or hut on stilts for the brakes man who operated a screw down jack in order to control the rate of descent of the loaded wagons on the incline.

The wagons, never more than eight at a time, were attached to a hemp rope (later a chain and later still an endless wire rope) which passed round an 18 foot diameter wooden drum with a perpendicular axle. When a disc signal at the bottom of the incline was rotated to the 'ready' position, the brakes man, having checked that the ganger had connected the loaded wagons to the rope, released the brake to allow the descent and ascent to begin.

From the top of 'The Plane' 'The Top Line' or upper section of the tramway led away to the quarries in Dove Holes Dale about two miles away. The loaded wagons had to be pulled by horses up to the highest point of the line about a quarter of a mile from the last of the Dove Holes quarries from where the wagons were run by gravity to the top of the incline.

The Walk

[1] Make your way eastwards from the Market Place along the main road to Buxton. About a third of a mile further on, just past the junction with the A624 road from Hayfield and Glossop, Ashbourne Lane goes off to the south east on your right. Go along this lane. Just after a slight bend to the right Moss Cottage (you may have noticed this house when looking up the incline on the previous walk) appears on the left. The Peak Forest Tramway's incline was immediately to the east of this cottage. Continue on along the lane as it climbs up the hill parallel to the incline.

[2] Near the top of the hill the lane bears slightly to the right away from the incline with some houses now appearing on the left. A worthwhile view of the course of the incline is to be had by going along the track which goes off to the left immediately south of Ashbourne Cottage and signposted significantly 'Top o' th' Plane' - the local name for the incline. Follow the track right up to the garage ahead and then turn sharp left. A few paces further on a right turn brings you onto the incline itself just below the top where the brakes man's tower was situated. If you go down the steps opposite you will get a good view of the stone revetted earthworks on top of which were laid the sidings for marshalling the wagons before being sent down the incline.

Now retrace your steps back as far as Ashbourne Lane. On the way back note the big stone building just to the south of the garage previously mentioned. This building was once the blacksmith's shop of of the Peak Forest Tramway.

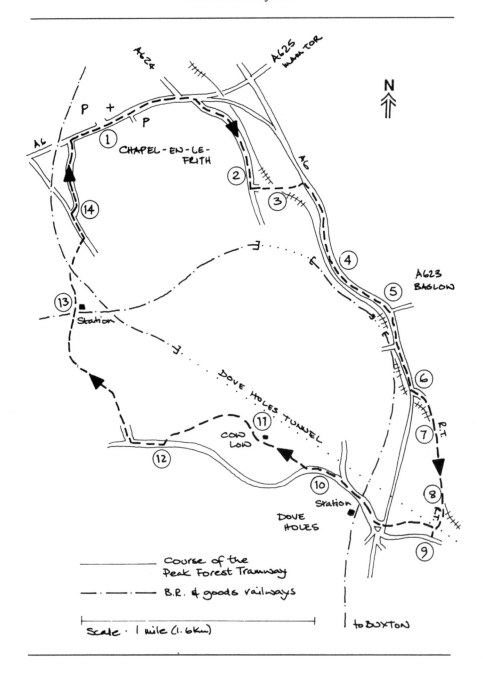

N

A24

A625 MAM TOR

P +
P

AL

① CHAPEL - EN - LE -
FRITH

②

③

A6

④

A623
BAGLOW

⑤

⑥

⑦

⑧

⑨

⑩

⑪

⑫

⑬ Station

⑭

Station
DOVE
HOLES

COW
LOW

DOVE HOLES TUNNEL

R.T.

to BUXTON

—————— Course of the
Peak Forest Tramway

— · — · — B.R. & goods railways

Scale · 1 mile (1.6km)

Once back on Ashbourne Lane proceed southwards for a few paces and then, just past the last house on your left, go east on the footpath which can be seen running between two low stone walls.

After about a 100 yards this path will give you a good view of the marshalling area at the top of the incline. The small stone building at the far side is reputed to have been one of the stables for the horses working the line. There was once a large set of stables immediately to the north west of this little one.

[3] The footpath goes straight on and crosses the course of the tramway at the point where it left the marshalling yard to move off to the south east towards Barmoor Clough. As you cross the tramway trackbed note the stone sleepers still in position.

Continue along the footpath as it goes straight downhill to the east. A wooden stile brings you out above the Chapel to Buxton road. Make your way down the slope and cross over carefully to the pavement on the other side. Walk south now along the road.

As you proceed the tramway trackbed can be seen emerging above on the western lip of Barmoor Clough. There was once a Barytes Works on the east side of the road. To serve this there was a siding on the tramway opposite. Coal for the works and other materials were tipped down chutes from the siding above down into road carts waiting below.

[4] The road soon draws level with the course of the tramway while on the far right the railway to Buxton joins the scene. The tramway continued on running between the road and the railway. A council road stores dump now occupies part of the trackbed here. Soon road, tramway and railway move apart, the railway cutting through a spur in the hillside by a tunnel while the tramway winds round it.

[5] Next you come to the junction of the A623 with the A6. Here, behind the houses on the south east side of the junction, was Loads Knowle Quarry which was the original destination of the tramway as built by Outram. The quarry was reached by a branch which reversed back from the later main line of the tramway crossing the Buxton road about 150 yards south of the road junction. The branch ended in a short incline leading up to the quarry itself. This incline was self-acting normally, but there was a horse gin fixed to a big wheel at the top of the incline in order to pull up empty wagons when no loaded wagons were ready to

go down. The trackbed of the incline and also of the branch as far as a stone wall on the east side of the Buxton road is quite well preserved.

From the road junction follow the A6 road to the south. Ahead, on the west side of the A6, is a double arched bridge carrying a lane over both the tramway (east arch) and the Buxton railway. A good view of the tramway formation is to be had from this bridge. South of the bridge the course of the tramway can be seen bending away from the railway to pass under the road to Buxton.

Trees bordering the course of the single track branch of the Peak Forest Tramway mask the damage done to the landscape by modern quarrying not far away.

[6] Back on the A6 continue on as far as the bridge carrying the road over the course of the tramway. Immediately to the north of this bridge and in front of the sign-board 'Dove Holes' is a farm road leading off to the south east. Follow this farm road for about 150 yards until you see a wooden pad stile on your right situated just to the left of a metal gate. (Be careful not to confuse this with a private bar stile just a few yards back - the stile you want is about 35 paces beyond the stone wall and line of old hawthorn trees coming down on your left.) Go over the stile and make your way diagonally across the field, aiming for the high wooden stile in the southern corner. Go over this stile and continue for a few yards along the top of the cutting above the course of the tramway and then drop down the slope to a third stile which is at the bottom and gives access to the tramway trackbed.

The path now follows the tramway trackbed as it bends to the south, past the remains of numerous limestone quarries. The first quarry on the left was Gisborne Quarry which, at its northern end, seems to have had what looks like a former incline running up to the face. In the trackbed of the tramway many stone sleepers remain. Note that some have two holes drilled, while others have three holes drilled.

[7] The course of the tramway now runs straight to the south through Dove Holes Dale proper. This part was reached by the tramway by 1800. No doubt then, and for many years afterwards, this would have been a very busy place, with the limestone being cut away from the quarry faces and the smoke rising from the many lime kilns dotted around. Somewhere about here was a long low shed with tramway track inside so that wagons loaded with lime could be stored overnight. This stopped the lime from getting wet and 'falling' or changing into quick lime.

[8] After about a quarter of a mile a fence made of old metal sheets lies across the trackbed. Pass through using the stile in the middle and go forward for about 50 places until you come to a gate on your right. The tramway split into several sections here; the main two branches going away for about a mile each to the south south east and the south east. Unfortunately, however, as you can see, modern quarrying has obliterated any trace of these. The trackbed of a minor single track branch to the south west, however, remains intact and it is that which the walk will follow.

Go through the gate on your right and pick up the trackbed of the branch as it begins to bend away to the south west of the left of a clump of trees after starting in front of the remains of the recently demolished house near the gate.

The course of the branch passes through an old quarry and then bends back to the south again to end at a gate giving access to the road from Dove Holes to Peak Dale.

[9] The high embankment to your right on both side of the road belonged to a later quarry railway and was not connected with the Peak Forest system. This then marks the end of the exploration of the remains of the Peak Forest Tramway.

Go back from the gate for about 25 paces and then turn off the trackbed of the tramway branch to the left (i.e. the west) and make your way up the slope to the wooden stile ahead. Cross over and follow the path as it goes westwards.

After about 80 paces the path divides. Take the left path crossing over the wooden stile near the fork. Keep straight onto the west going past the children's playground on your left to reach the main road passing through the village of Dove Holes. Cross over the main road and go straight ahead on the minor road leading off to the west opposite. Turn right at the road junction after about 100 yards onto the road that goes north westwards to cross over the railway to Buxton next to Dove Holes Station.

[10] About 200 yards west of the railway bridge turn left up the lane that goes off north westwards.

(The next section of the walk goes through a farmyard and can be muddy at times though there are some fine views. If you do not fancy this simply keep on along the lane for a further three-quarters of a mile and rejoin the walk at point 12 next to the plantation of trees on your right).

About 80 yards after the last house on the north side of the lane on your right is a stile in the wall. Cross over and proceed as follows. Go over the stile few yards to the west - cross the field bearing slightly to the right, aiming for the gate - go through the gate and aim for the farmhouse ahead - go over the stile just east of the farmhouse - proceed on in front of the farmhouse - bear left round the new barn in front and then keep going right until you emerge in the farmyard where you turn left.

[11] Just out of the farmyard go to the right leaving the farm road to follow the trackway that runs downhill to the north west. After about 150 yards, as the dip starts to turn into a valley, go off to the left to pass round the hill of Cow Low on your left. Soon a pleasant green terraced way appears. On your right is a fine view which includes two operating railways. Deep down below is the former Midland line preparing to dive into Dove Holes Tunnel, while over it passes the former London and North Western Line as it approaches Chapel-en-le-Frith Station.

Follow the path as it straightens out to run south west until (after four stiles) it meets the tarmac road at the north end of a hardwood plantation.

[12] Turn right and go to the west along the road for about 250 yards until, after the first field beyond the plantation, a stone surfaced road appears on your right leading down hill in a north westerly direction. Follow this stone surfaced road downhill (keeping left at all junctions) until you come to Chapel-en-le-Frith Station. Cross over the railway and go over the stile next to the gate straight ahead. Follow the trackway you find yourself on, travelling northwards until it joins the road from the station. Go along this road and then turn left at the first junction into Long Lane.

The quickest way back into the centre of Chapel-en-le-Frith is to turn right off Long Lane on the road leading off to the north west just before the bridge taking the former Midland line over your road. Then go second left and you will soon find yourself on the main road through Chapel where a right turn will bring you back to the start of the walk.

Walk 7: The Cromford and High Peak Railway:Whaley Bridge to Bunsall and the Fernilee Reservoir Railway

Map: Pathfinder Maps 742 SK 08/18 and 760 SK 07/17 or Outdoor Leisure Maps 1 'The Peak District Dark Peak Area' and 24 'The Peak District White Peak Area'.

Distance: just over 8 miles

Start: The canal basin on the north side of Whaley Bridge. Grid reference SK 012 816.

By Car: Whaley Bridge can easily be reached from the A6 Stockport to Buxton road turning off to the south at the round-about at the western end of the Whaley Bridge to Chapel-en-le-Frith by-pass about $3/4$ of a mile south of Furness Vale. The canal basin is just below the east side of the main road through the town and can be reached by taking the first turning off to the left when approaching from the north. Just past the canal basin immediately to the south east of the old warehouse is a public car park.

By Public Transport: The BR station for Whaley Bridge, just opposite the canal basin, is served by a regular service of trains from Manchester, Stockport and Buxton.

This walk explores the first part of the western end of the Cromford and High Peak Railway, taking the railway explorer through the attractive and popular Goyt Valley. The walk also covers the remains of the Fernilee Reservoir Railway. Not too difficult underfoot, though some sections can be muddy after wet weather. The only steep climb is on the road parallel to the Shallcross Incline.

The Railways

The desire to link by some means or other the Cromford Canal in the east to the nearest canal head on the west side of the hills of the Derbyshire Peak District was not given up when the Peak Forest project provided nothing more than a tramway feeder to the canal system on the west side of the hills (see pages 50/51). Further efforts to provide this link centred on, once again, a canal crossing the hills of northern Derbyshire. The problems, however, of building a canal to link the Cromford Canal to the Peak Forest Canal were considerable as a climb to over 1,200 feet above sea-level was envisaged and water supply problems on the dry limestone uplands loomed large. In view of all this, the trans Peak canal scheme was abandoned and a tramway scheme running on approximately the same course substituted.

The first Act concerning this project, dated 2 May 1825, spoke of the proposal as 'a Railway or Tramroad for the passage of waggons and other carriages, to be propelled thereon by Stationary or Locomotive Steam Engines or other sufficient power'. The first section of the Cromford and High Peak Railway, as the line was named, to be opened was that from Cromford Wharf to the bottom of Hurdlow Incline. This came into use on 29 May 1830. The remaining section, covering the rest of the line to Whaley Bridge, opened on 6 July 1831.

The total length of the Cromford and High Peak Railway, often known simply as the High Peak Railway, was 33 miles when fully opened, of which 28 miles was single line and five miles double line. Of the latter, three miles was on incline, thus leaving only two miles of double track on the level. This seems to indicate that much of the level trackbed formation of the High Peak Railway, which these walks will explore and which are clearly double, have been subject to a later, though probably early, alteration. The original track consisted of cast iron, fish-bellied rails laid on chairs which were pegged to roughly squared stone sleepers.

There were originally seven inclines on the High Peak Railway, three on the west side and four on the east side. Of these one on the east (Cromford - Sheep Pasture) and one on the west (Bunsall) were worked in two sections. All these inclines, with the exception in later years of the short one at Whaley Bridge (see below), were powered by stationary beam engines, all supplied by the Butterly Company. Originally all the inclines were equipped with endless chains. After 1855 many of the chains were replaced by hemp rope and later still by wire rope. Accidents with wagons breaking free on inclines were common. For instance, there were no less than four accidents with runaway wagons on the Shallcross Incline between 1859 and 1864.

The level sections between the inclines were at first worked by horses. In fact, in the early days the Cromford and High Peak Railway Company simply acted as proprietors of the line with all the traffic being worked by private carriers using their own horses and wagons. The traffic in the early days, which was minerals and goods only, was slow moving. It is said that it took about two days for a wagon to travel from one end of the line to the other. In 1833 a horse-drawn passenger coach, operated by a private carrier, began to run on the line.

It was also in 1833 that the High Peak Railway acquired its first steam engine which was an 0-4-0 (almost certainly tender) engine named 'Peak' and built by Robert Stephenson and Co. of Newcastle. The introduction of locomotives continued only slowly. For instance, it was not until 1857 that the first locomotive worked on the level section between the top of Shallcross Incline and the bottom of Bunsall Incline. In 1860 private traders were given one month's notice to cease working their horses on the line so as to enable all traffic to be worked by the High Peak Railway Company's locomotives.

Meanwhile the skeleton passenger service of apparently no more than one coach each day continued. An eyewitness description in 1854 tells us that the service was provided by a horse-drawn carriage carrying 16 people inside and 14 people outside. The passengers apparently stayed in the carriage while it went up and down the inclines. The journey of 32 miles took four hours. By 1858 the company rule book forbade the carrying of passengers up and down the inclines so presumably anybody travelling the whole length of the line would have had to get out and walk no less than seven times! By this time also it appears that the passenger service consisted simply of a brake van with passenger accommodation attached to the rear of a goods train and known as the 'fly'. The length of time taken to cover the line increased considerably. For instance, in July 1862 a 'fly' which left Cromford at 9.00 a.m. had only got to the foot of Bunsall Incline by 5.15 p.m., with still several miles to go before the terminus at Whaley Bridge would be reached. We are told that on this occasion there were two passengers on board. The passenger service, not surprisingly, ended in 1876 or 1877.

The section of the High Peak Railway which this walk will cover extends from the western terminus at the canal basin to the foot of Bunsall Incline about three-and-a-half miles away. On this section there were two inclines. The first of these was the Whaley Bridge Incline (180 yards, 1 in $13^1/_2$ gradient) which was originally worked by horses. In 1833 it was agreed that a stationary engine should be installed and this was duly done. In 1886 or soon afterwards, however, horse working was resumed when a horse capstan was installed. This continued in use until the incline with the railway to the canal yard closed in 1952.

On the level section of about half a mile of line between the top of Whaley Bridge Incline and the bottom of Shallcross Incline, approximately half way along, a link was installed in 1857 to the newly opened Stockport, Disley and Whaley Bridge Railway. After the Shallcross Incline (817 yards, 1 in 101/4 gradient) there follows a longer level of about two-and-a-quarter miles to the foot of Bunsall Incline which is as far as this walk follows the High Peak line.

It was on one of the inclines near Whaley Bridge, probably on the Whaley Bridge Incline itself, that John Barraclough Fell (1815 - 1902) laid track of three feet seven and three-eighths inches gauge to test his centre rail friction drive system which he had devised for use on the railway over the Mont Cenis Pass in the Alps. Although this railway did not last long (it was planned only as a stop gap until the Mont Cenis Tunnel opened), Fell's system came to be used on several steeply graded railways in different parts of the world.

With the exception of the first short part as far as Shallcross Yard, all of the western section of the High Peak Railway north of Ladmanlow near Buxton was abandoned on 25 June 1892 as an alternative better graded route via Buxton, avoiding the use of expensive to operate inclines, was now available. Also there was no locally generated mineral traffic, as on the eastern and central sections, to justify retention. This, however, was not the end of the use of railways in the Goyt Valley.

In 1932 Stockport Corporation started work on building a large earth dam across the Goyt Valley at Fernilee. The main contractors, Lehane, Mackenzie and Shand Ltd., first of all laid a two foot gauge railway along the level section of the trackbed of the High Peak Railway that ran beside the east side of the future reservoir in order to enable a high pressure pipe to be laid. This two foot gauge railway may also have served a small quarry opened out on the east side of the future reservoir. Two 0-4-0 saddle tank locomotives are known to have been used on this system.

Soon, however, a more substantial three foot gauge railway was laid down with much of the track and stock coming from Lehane's contract at Gorple in Yorkshire (see Walk 2). This three foot gauge system was as not as long as some reservoir railways. The puddle field was only a quarter of a mile from the dam site on the eastern side of the valley, while the major quarry served by the system, Issue Tor Quarry, was situated also just a quarter of a mile away from the construction site, though high up on the hillside on the west side of the valley. The railway reached the quarry via a double track self-acting incline.

The locomotive shed was situated just north east of the eastern end of the future wall. At least 15 three foot gauge steam locomotives (three 0-4-0 well tank, nine 0-4-0 saddle tank, one 0-6-0 saddle tank and two 0-6-0 side [wing] tank; all with outside cylinders) are known to have worked at Fernilee. Unlike some other reservoir railway systems, the one at Fernilee had no 'Paddy Mail' service, though there was a saloon coach which was presumably used for transporting civic dignitaries around the site.

The works were declared 'open' on 10 June 1937, though there were still engines at the shed in November of that year. The railway was probably lifted soon afterwards.

The Walk

Before setting off, it is worthwhile exploring the canal basin. Here goods were transhipped between the railway and the canal. The original stone transhipment sheds remain. A glimpse at the bottom of the south door of the westernmost of the two sheds will reveal a section of rail still in place between the stone setts.

[1] From the south east corner of the easternmost transhipment shed set off southwards on the tarmac road that runs between the car park and the stone building to the south of the canal basin. This road is laid on the trackbed of the High Peak Railway.

You soon arrive at a metal railway bridge over the River Goyt. This bridge, which replaced the earlier stone bridge of the High Peak line has recently been opened to pedestrians. Proceed over the bridge. As you cross, note how sensibly the authorities have preserved the (later) railway track in the bed of the footway.

Immediately over the bridge, straight ahead, a well laid out footpath

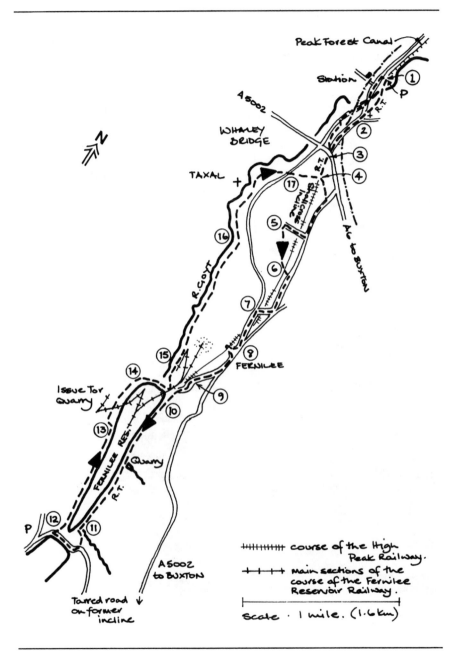

ascends straight up the slope to the south. This footpath is on the course of the Whaley Bridge Incline which was the shortest on the whole of the High Peak Railway, being only 180 yards long and rising at a gradient of 1 in $13^1/_2$. Ascend the path to the top of the incline trackbed.

At the top, where the path flattens out, you enter a wide, roughly circular enclosure. Here the wagons would be hitched and unhitched before going down or coming up the incline. In the circular area a horse was harnessed to one end of a wooden beam which was bolted to the top of a vertical spindle which, via a pinion and gear wheel, drove a horizontal pulley. Round this passed the chain to which the wagons on

This attractively resurfaced former railway bridge, on the site of the original bridge, invites the walker to begin his or her exploration of the Cromford and High Peak Railway.

the incline were attached. Here also was once sited the stationary steam engine which worked the incline from 1834 to soon after 1886 when the horse capstan was installed.

Proceed southwards along the footpath which lies between walls wide enough for double rail tracks to be laid.

[2] In about 50 yards the path ends at a tarmac road. Ahead the High Peak Railway the course now lies covered by a private road and some works buildings. Beyond these the High Peak Railway passed under the later railway to Buxton by a low bridge now filled in.

Turn left on the tarmac road and follow it as it bends round to the south. Soon the houses on the right end and there is a good view of the Stockport to Buxton Railway. On the far side and below this later railway the course of the High Peak Railway can be clearly seen.

[3] When the old main road to Buxton is reached turn right. Almost immediately you find yourself on the bridge taking this road over the course of the High Peak Railway. Cross over and go down the steps on the south side of the road which take you down to the trackbed of the High Peak ''ne and proceed southwards.

Just before some flats are reached a stone plaque with a section of original fish-bellied type rail fastened nearby reminds passers-by of the High Peak Railway. Note that, unlike a section of modern rail, the ends of a fish-bellied rail differ. This was so that each section could be slotted into the section beyond.

The flats beyond lie on the course of the High Peak Railway line, so take the tarmac path to their left. Follow this path between the stream and the flats until it turns right to bring you out into a large open space.

Here the wagons were marshalled before being sent up the Shallcross Incline (817 yards long and graded at 1 in $10^1/_4$) which set off up the hillside ahead, just past the large metal bollard which was used in connection with wagon shunting here.

Unfortunately, the incline has been built over further up so it is not possible to ascend it.

[4] Bear left, taking the tarmac lane that runs to the south west between a stone house on the north side and the big red brick Kenfab works building on the south side. After about 300 yards bear right on the road

that comes in on your left across the stream. Follow this road uphill to the south for about 400 yards until, on your right, in the middle of an estate of houses, you reach Shallcross Road. Go west along Shallcross Road for just over 100 yards.

The last estate house on each side of the road has been built on the course of the incline. Just beyond these two houses the course of the incline can be easily made out from the road as it climbs up the hill. Could the raised ground to the north and immediately to the west of the incline about halfway down be for out of control wagon escape? To the south the top of Shallcross Incline can be made out just to the left of a large mound on the horizon.

[5] Continue west along Shallcross Road for about 150 yards until you reach, on your left just before some houses, a wooden gap stile. Cross over into a field and, turning sharp left, climb upwards to the south east, keeping to the left of the row of trees in the field and aiming to reach the ridge beyond just to the right of the mound at the top of the incline.

On reaching the brow of the hill you should have a good view of the Goyt Valley, with the course of the High Peak Railway clearly visible as it runs along the contour to the south. Walk straight on, aiming for the gap stile in the west boundary wall of the tramway trackbed, just before two prominent stone gate posts jutting out from the same boundary wall. To the north east the top of the incline with the dam for supplying water to the stationary engine can be seen.

[6] On reaching this stile look west and you will see what appears to be the course of a short branch tramway bearing away from the High Peak Railway in a curve to the remains of a pit to the south west.

Go through the wall onto the High Peak Railway trackbed and walk southwards for a few yards until you come to a metal gate on your left. Go through the gap at the side of the gate and make for the gap stile in the south east corner of the field you find yourself in. Go through this and turn right on the tarmac lane.

Walk south for about a quarter of a mile along this lane, which runs roughly parallel to the course of the High Peak Railway. Opposite a rough surfaced lane coming in on your left, turn right to go downhill down a narrow tarmac lane.

[7] The High Peak Railway crossed this lane near the bottom. Garages have been erected on the trackbed on both side of the lane. At the junction of the lane with the Whaley Bridge to Buxton road turn left.

Soon the course of the railway appears running in a cutting on your left. The main road now goes straight across the course of the railway but formerly it bent round to the right and then sharp left to cross the railway on a stone bridge, just past the National Park sign. The south side of this is still partly visible.

[8] About 250 yards further on along the main road turn right into the trackway (public footpath sign) that goes off downhill to the west immediately to the south of the first house on the right. Follow the track down under the stone bridge which once carried the High Peak Railway over the lane. Note that the bridge is made for a double track railway. Continue along the trackway as it bears sharp left to cross a stream. A glance to the left will reveal the high embankment of the High Peak Railway as it crosses the clough.

A few yards up the bank on the other side of the stream, turn sharp left immediately past the first house on the left onto another trackway. Go east on this trackway.

Soon the course of the High Peak Railway is crossed again but this time on the level. Less than 100 yards further on the main road is met again. Turn right on this and go south until, after about 150 yards, you come to the road going down to Fernilee Reservoir on your right. Proceed down this road.

[9] A little way down, through the trees on your right, a stone wall can be seen. The High Peak Railway used to run on the other side of this wall. Follow the road as it bends left and then right, noting as you go the railway embankment on your right. After the bend to the right the road crosses the course of the railway on the level. Somewhere about here was the shed which once housed the 15 or so three foot gauge locomotives that worked on Fernilee Reservoir project in the 1930s. Later landscaping has obscured any trace of the three foot railway round about here but you will be able to see evidence of it on the return walk.

Take the left-hand road which heads off to the south to run alongside the east side of Fernilee Reservoir. The High Peak Railway ran on what is now the grass verge on your left. Note the east side of the former railway cutting - the west side having been removed during the construction of the reservoir.

[10] Before long the tarmac road ends and a stile gives access to the High Peak Railway trackbed which from here on has been left undisturbed. It was along here that a two foot gauge (soon superseded by a three foot gauge) railway was laid during the early days of the reservoir construction, 1932/33. The course of the railway curves a little to the left to pass through a cutting after which it runs along the lake side. The scene with the flat expanse of water on the right now looks very different from what it must have looked like when the High Peak Railway ran along here, hugging the side of what was then a quite deep valley.

Further south are the remains of a small quarry which may have been served by the two foot railway. Then a substantial embankment, now mostly submerged, is crossed.

[11] Near the southern end of the reservoir another stile gives you access to a tarmac road which soon turns to the left to climb south eastwards uphill. Here you are at the bottom of the course of the long Bunsall Incline. When the High Peak Railway opened it was worked as two separate inclines. The lower end and shorter section was 455 yards long with gradient of 1 in 7, while the upper one was 660 yards long with a 1 in $7^1/_2$ gradient.

Follow the road as it runs uphill on the trackbed of the incline. Someway up the hill the road turns off to the right, leaving the course of the incline which continues straight on in a cutting now filled with trees. A short climb up the grass bank on the right-hand side of the cutting will reveal the remains of a filled in stone bridge which carried an old trackway over the railway.

This is as far as this walk takes you along the High Peak Railway. The suggested return route will, however, give some worthwhile and different views of the course of the railway as well as enabling you to see some of the visible remains of the Fernilee Reservoir Railway.

Cross over to the west side of the Goyt Valley on the top of the dam wall of the Errwood Reservoir just to the south west of you. At the western end of the reservoir wall there is a view of the upper part of the

[12] At the end of the retaining wall turn right off the road and take the path that drops gently down the slope in a northerly direction towards the western side of Fernilee Reservoir. Follow the path as it makes its way northwards along the west side of the reservoir.

[13] About two-thirds of the way along the side of the reservoir the path leaves the side of the reservoir to climb up the slope through the trees until it reaches a trackway running north roughly parallel to the reservoir but at a higher level. Turn right and follow this trackway northwards until, on your right, you come to a clearance in the trees with wire fencing placed round to prevent people from falling into a gully caused by a landslip.

Immediately after this opening, on your left, you will see a small stone embankment, with birch trees on it, dropping down to the trackway. This is part of the remains of the three foot gauge double track self-acting incline which led from Issue Tor Quarry higher up the hill to the reservoir works below.

A worthwhile diversion for the energetic is to follow the course of the incline uphill through the trees and then through somewhat more open terrain on a substantial embankment formed of tumbled stone (note no right of way but the woods are Forestry Commission). At the top is the quarry with an impressive face with large tumbled blocks of stone lying at its base. Return the same way to the trackway.

Back on the trackway thick planting of fir trees prevents observation of the remains of the incline below it to the east. Resume your walk to the north along the trackway.

[14] Where the woods end cross over the stile, turn right and make your way down the trackway that leads towards the retaining wall of Fernilee Reservoir. From the trackway, if you look back to your right, you will have a good overall view of the Bunsall Incline (a tarmac road runs on its upper section).

When you reach the reservoir retaining wall don't cross over but take the track that leads off north (notice at the side 'No unauthorised parking beyond this point').

Soon you find that you have a good view of the course of the High Peak Railway as it runs between the hamlet of Fernilee and the reservoir, hugging the eastern side of the valley. Also from here you can observe the course of the three foot gauge reservoir railway, also on the opposite of the valley, as it runs northwards from the east end of the retaining wall to the puddle clayfield site a quarter of a mile away to the north, The three foot puddle field branch left the course of the High Peak Railway just by the modern house which you can see at the bottom of the fir trees just to the north of the east end of the retaining wall. It can be observed running in a straight line dropping gently downhill diagonally across the slope to the disturbed ground where the puddle field was sited.

Make your way back to the retaining wall of the reservoir and cross over to the east side. Go left here down the road that leads past the filter house. Beyond the filter house take the green trackway that leads off to the north in the bottom of the valley on the east side of the river.

[15] Just past the filter house on your right you will see a terraced out way gently dropping down the steep bank of the lower section of the valley from the north towards the filter house. This could well be the trackbed of the reservoir railway as it came down via a reversal neck to the site of the filter house.

Further down the valley the green trackway fades away and you find yourself on a field path. This however, is easy to follow as it keeps close to the east bank of the river for a mile beyond the filter house.

[16] Where the river bends a little to the west the path does not run along the bank but at the bottom of Shallcross Wood on the east side of the flat area in the valley bottom.

At the north end of the Shallcross Wood two wicket gates lead you across the old trackway leading down left to a ford and the village of Taxal beyond. Continue north through the second wicket gate. Follow the footpath as it bends a little to the right to join a stone surfaced trackway coming in on the left. Follow the trackway until it reaches the main road to the north east.

[17] Cross the main road and proceed along Mevril Road opposite. After the last house on the right make your way across the playing field to join a footpath which starts off downhill to the north east immediately to the right of the high wire fence on the east side of the playing field.

Make your way down the path which runs on what appears to have been a short branch incline which, at the bottom, connected with the

High Peak Railway. At the bottom you find yourself back at the foot of the Shallcross Incline. Retrace your walk past the flats onto the course of the High Peak Railway which you followed on your way out.

When you get to the road bridge over the railway trackbed do not go off on the path to the left but continue on along the railway trackbed until public way ends at the point where the High Peak Railway originally went under the Whaley Bridge to Buxton railway. Here a path leads left onto the Buxton to Whaley Bridge road. Turn right on the road and you will soon be back at the start of the walk.

Walk 8: The Cromford and High Peak Railway: Bunsall to Ladmanlow

Map: Pathfinder Map 760 SK 07/17 or Outdoor Leisure Map 24 'The Peak District White Peak Area'.

Distance: $5^1/_2$ miles.

Start: The car park situated in the Goyt Valley just north east of the northern end of the Errwood Reservoir. Grid reference SK 018 758.

By Car: Take the road to the Goyt valley which branches off to the south at the south western end of Kettleshulme Village from the A5002 Whaley Bridge to Macclesfield road. Two miles south of Kettleshulme turn left at the T-junction and go down into the Goyt Valley. Near the bottom of the valley take the left-hand road which crosses the valley on the retaining wall of the Errwood Reservoir. The car park (with toilet block) is on the left about 200 yards from the east end of the retaining wall.

By Public Transport: Those arriving by train at Buxton can pick up the walk at its half-way point $1^1/_2$ miles south west of Buxton. From Buxton Station walk south westwards along the A54 road to Congleton as far as Burbage. Here just past the parish church of Christ Church leave the main road by keeping right and going up the road to Ann Croft. $2/_3$ mile up this road the walk can be picked up at point 9 where the course of the High Peak Railway is crossed over by the road which by this point has become an unmetalled way.

This walk is over the hills round Burbage Edge between Buxton and the Goyt Valley, following the remains and relics of the Cromford and High Peak Valley on what was its loneliest section.

The Railway

An outline of the origins of the High Peak Railway can be found in the introduction to the previous walk.

The section of the High Peak Railway which will be covered by this walk starts near the bottom of the Bunsall Incline. Originally this incline was worked as two separate inclines (lower one 455 yards, gradient 1 in 7; upper one 660 yards, gradient 1 in $7^1/_2$). Working as one incline began on 8 June 1857. The incline, like all of those on the High Peak Railway, was power-assisted by a stationary steam engine.

From the top of Bunsall Incline there was a long, almost level, section as far as Hurdlow some nine miles away. About one mile from the incline top the railway entered Burbage Tunnel which, at 580 yards, was easily the longest on the line. The walk takes the railway explorer to within sight of Ladmanlow some two miles beyond the southern mouth of the tunnel.

The section of the High Peak Railway which is explored by this walk, was originally as busy as the central and eastern section which survived much longer. In 1874, for instance, there were at least ten train trips scheduled from Ladmanlow to Shallcross Yard (Whaley Bridge). By 1891, however, it seems that there was only one scheduled train a day over the section of line west of Ladmanlow. In 1892 the line between Ladmanlow and Shallcross Yard was abandoned with the track being lifted by 1894.

The Walk

[1] Just below the north west end of the car park is the entrance to the bridge which once carried the High Peak Railway under the bridleway leading off to the north east. The eastern end of the bridge has completely disappeared under earth fill.

Set off to the south east on the tarmac road which, as the notice on the right side of the road tells us, was laid on the course of Bunsall Incline in 1967.

[2] About 200 yards uphill, on your left, you will come to the remains of a small rectangular shaped dam. Between this dam and the road there is an area of flat ground. This was the top of the lower section of the Bunsall Incline when it was worked in two sections up until 1857. Note a pit, probably the wheel pit, and the foundations of a small square shaped building nearer the road. Somewhere here there would have been an engine house because the incline was worked by a stationary engine and also probably a brakes man's hut. No doubt the small dam was there to provide a water supply for the stationary steam engine.

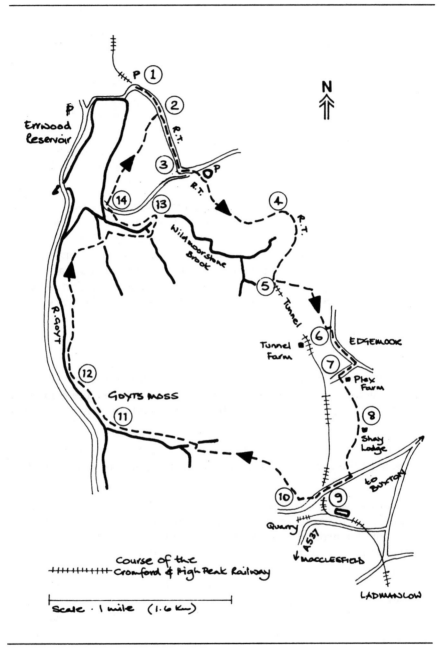

N

Errwood
Reservoir

R.T.

P (1)
(2)
(3)
(4)
(5)
(6) EDGEMOOR
(7)
(8) Shay Lodge
(9)
(10)
(11)
(12)
(13)
(14)

Wildmoorstone Brook

R. Goyt

GOYTS MOSS

Tunnel

Tunnel Farm

Plex Farm

to Buxton

Quarry

A537

↓ MACCLESFIELD

LADMANLOW

Course of the
++++++++++ Cromford & High Peak Railway

Scale · 1 mile (1.6 Km)

Look to the south east and you can make out the start of the upper section of the earlier incline disappearing under the curving embankment of the later single incline which now has the tarmac road on it.

Continue on uphill on the course of the incline.

After about 100 yards you come to a point where an old way once passed underneath the incline embankment via a round arched stone bridge. The western side of this bridge is still visible below the right-hand side of the embankment.

Continue following the course of the incline by going uphill, either on the tarmac road or on the rough ground on the right-hand side.

[3] Near the brow of the hill the course of the incline enters a cutting and then quickly levels off bearing round to the left. By the start of the bend, on the right, note the flat area of ground where the engine winding house for the Bunsall Incline may well have been sited.

These two parallel curved embankments (at point 4 on the walk) are an unusual feature on the Cromford and High Peak Railway.

After the bend the course of the railway begins a long level run as it crosses Goyt's Lane and proceeds south eastwards over a high embankment which doubles as a dam wall. This dam, no doubt, would have once supplied water for the boiler of the steam-powered winding engine.

There is no right of way along the course of the High Peak Railway here but, as the trackbed is freely used by the public, the suggested walk continues that way.

After leaving the embankment the course of the railway is easy to follow as it bends to the left round the side of Wild Moor. Round the bend you have one of the most impressive bits of pre-inter-city railway engineering in England as the course of the railway bends round in a big loop on a series of substantial embankments high up on the moors.

[4] Where the course of the railway starts to make its first right-hand bend in the big loop you come to the strange phenomenon of two separate but parallel embankments built next to each other. It seems that the northern embankment was built first and that later, when the line was doubled, the southern embankment was made as an alternative to widening the older embankment with its sharper curve.

If you examine the surface of the northern embankment you will be able to see a number of stone sleepers buried in the surface. They all have a single hole drilled to fasten the chair. Most seem to be of grit or sandstone but at least one limestone one can be noted. The south most embankment, it will be noted, has a stone revetted top section.

[5] Continue on along the course of the railway until you come to a left-hand bend and the blocked entrance of Burbage Tunnel (580 yards long) comes into view. Note how on the bend the trackbed surface is much wider than normal suggesting there were once sidings here.

The tunnel portal, unfortunately, has collapsed or has been dismantled so that the present blocking is fixed a little back from the original entrance. Note how the tunnel mouth is set forward from and is not situated at the back of the cutting as one might expect. Why was this? Perhaps there was a fear of landslips at the end of the cutting.

To pick up the course of the High Peak Railway on the other side of the hill it is necessary to take the footpath that leads away from the line about 100 yards north of the tunnel entrance. The path runs at the side of a tumbled wall which goes up the slope in an easterly direction starting from the railway boundary wall on the north side of the stream.

Near the brow of the hill the wall turns to the north. Here the path leaves the wall and goes across the moor in a south easterly direction. Posts with a yellow spot on the top mark the way.

The path next drops downhill to a wooden stile at the southern end of the wood ahead. Straight ahead you have a good view of the course of the High Peak Railway as it strikes southwards towards Ladmanlow. The south exit of the tunnel is situated below the house and barn (significantly named 'Tunnel Farm') which you can see on your right to the south east. Unfortunately, the tunnel portal is not visible from the path.

[6] Cross the stile and make your way downhill until you come to a stile giving you access to a lane. Cross over, turn right and follow the lane until, after about 400 yards, you come to some white gates across the lane with a lodge house on the left. Turn right up the farm road which branches off to the south west immediately on the other side of the white gates.

[7] After about 200 yards and just past the house on your left (Plex Farm) go through the gate on your left and take the track that leads between the house and the barn situated to the south west of the house. After passing through the gate that takes you out of the farmyard continue straight on (to the south west) to a stile in a stone wall to the left of the gate ahead. Next aim for the middle of the wood ahead.

A gap stile in the corner of the field gives access to the woods. Follow the path through the middle of the woods to a stone stile in the wall at the other side. Cross over and go on in a southerly direction, keeping to the right of the stone wall which leads away from the woods.

[8] Two more stiles bring you to a field with a small stone house on the other side ahead of you. Cross the field, making for the left side of the house. Here two gap stiles give you access to a trackway which leads off to the south. Follow this trackway, passing Shay Lodge Farm on your left. Soon you will be able to see an embankment which once carried the High Peak Railway above you across the fields on the right.

At the end of the track turn right onto the tarmac road which soon becomes a stone surfaced way leading uphill to the south west.

[9] After about 300 yards on this road you come to the point where the High Peak Railway passed under the road in what seems more like a short tunnel than a bridge. The northern portal has been filled in but the southern portal is still clear. From here you can observe the course of the High Peak Railway running over a high embankment and bending round to the south east to reach the former depot of Ladmanlow just beyond.

On the far side of the embankment the remains of a short branch leading off to a quarry a little way to the west can be seen. A short diversion through the gate ahead will give you a good view of this branch as it runs up to the quarry on a stone revetted embankment.

This is as far as this walk goes in exploring the High Peak Railway. The suggested route back starts by taking the path which leads off to the west from the road you are on immediately south west of the point where it goes over the trackbed of the High Peak Railway. The path is signposted 'Lamaload via Shining Tor'.

[10] At the end of the plantation on your right be careful not to go straight on but to turn right and go uphill to the north west gradually bearing away from the plantation. The path, which is well trodden and easy to follow, goes over the brow of the hill (stile) and drops down gently into the Goyt valley beyond.

[11] On reaching the footbridge over the River Goyt, unless you wish to go back to the car park at the start of the walk via the tarmac road that runs down the west side of the valley, don't cross over but go to the north following the well used way-marked path '6' which runs on the east side of river.

[12] At the next bridge, which is opposite Goyt Quarry, again don't cross over but keep to the east side of the river this time following way-marked path '4'.

This path is well used and well way-marked so only the following needs to be noted. When you turn eastwards up the valley of the Wildmoorstone Brook high above you to the north east you will see the embankment of the High Peak Railway which you walked on earlier.

[13] When you cross the Wildmoorstone Brook go left on the track that leads westwards on the north side of the valley.

locomotion was introduced for, in 1892, much of the course of the railway between Ladmanlow and Harpur Hill was realigned by the London and North Western Railway who by now owned the High Peak Railway. In the same year the High Peak Railway west of Ladmanlow was closed and a new link was opened between Buxton, Hindlow and Harpur Hill. This new link enabled the considerable amount of locally produced mineral traffic to go out to the main rail network avoiding the expensive to operate inclines to the west.

On 1 June 1894 the new line east of Hindlow through Hindlow Tunnel was opened thus enabling the old twisting route of the High Peak Railway between Harpur Hill and Hurdlow to be abandoned except for the first half mile at the Harpur Hill end which was retained in order that trains could still get to Hillhead Quarry.

The former LNWR's line between Hindlow and Ladmanlow which, for some of the way, at least, ran on the trackbed of the original High Peak Railway, lasted until well into this century. In 1954 the Ladmanlow Goods Depot was closed and the line from Hindlow cut back to the Mines Safety Research Station at Old Harpur. By 1973 all traffic west of Hindlow had ceased.

The Walk

[1] Make your way eastwards out of the car park and up the wide path signposted 'Poole's Cavern and Solomon's Temple'. At the top of the bank turn right and follow the path that leads westwards across an embankment over the upper part of the quarry. The quarry, now partly filled in, was served by a short branch line from the High Peak Railway as will be seen further on.

Go over the stile just past the west end of the embankment which gives access to an open grass ridge. From this ridge to the south you have a good view of the course of Cromford and High Peak Railway as it winds round roughly following the contour in a big loop. The high and prominent embankment which you can see just to the east of south belongs to the 1892 realigned line and not to the original High Peak Railway.

Keeping on to the west, cross the road leading to the picnic car park and aim for the wood stile beyond.

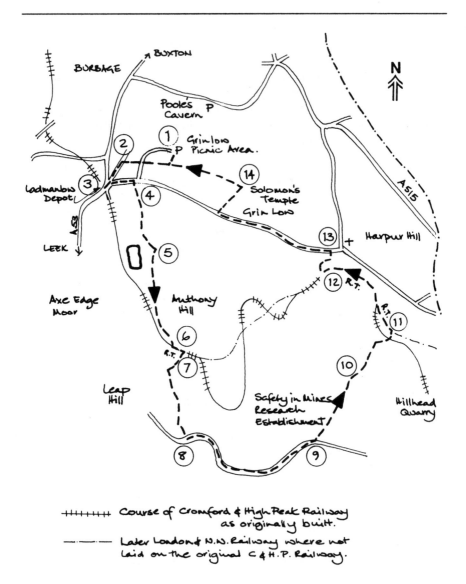

BURBAGE

BUXTON

Poole's P
Cavern

① Grinlow
P Picnic Area.

②

③ Ladmanlow Depot

LEEK

A53

④

⑤

⑥

⑦ R.T.

Axe Edge Moor

Anthony Hill

Leap Hill

⑧

⑨

Safety in Mines Research Establishment

⑩

⑪

⑫ R.T.

⑬ Harpur Hill

⑭ Solomon's Temple
Grin Low

A515

Hillhead Quarry

N

++++++++ Course of Cromford & High Peak Railway
as originally built.

—·——·—— Later London & N.W. Railway where not
laid on the original C & H.P. Railway.

Scale · 1 mile. (1.6 km)

[2] From here you have a good overall view of the course of the High Peak Railway from the south end of the Burbage Tunnel round to the site of Ladmanlow depot. Unfortunately, even in winter, trees hide the southern exit of Burbage Tunnel, which is just below Tunnel Farm which you can see on the hillside one-and-a-quarter miles away to the north west. The course of the railway, however, can easily be made out from there onwards making a fairly straight run to the south of just over half a mile and then running on an embankment and bending to the east to cross the road to Macclesfield. The bridge over the road has gone but the abutments remain, though what is left looks like 1892 work rather than original High Peak Railway work.

Drop down the slope, cross the stile at the bottom (in front of the stone shed) and go left on the trackway leading away to the south west.

[3] The trackway ends at the junction of the road to Harpur Hill with the Buxton to Leek road. Immediately west of the road junction and on the north west side of the Leek road are the remains of Ladmanlow Goods Depot with the crossing keeper's house still remaining; the High Peak Railway here having, of course, crossed the road on the level.

On the opposite side of the road the course of the High Peak Railway (not here realigned in 1892) can be seen running straight for half a mile in a southerly direction and now tarmacked over. Just in front of the gate with the Health and Safety Executive notice barring entry to the public, the Clay Cross Company's Grin Quarry branch led off to the east bending round behind the terraced houses beyond.

Make your way east from the road junction for about 300 yards as far as the last two houses on the south side of the road.

[4] At about the point where the road to the picnic place leaves the road to Harpur Hill the Grin Quarry branch crossed over the road on the level. Now go south along the trackway that leads off the Harpur Hill road between the last two houses on the south side of the road (footpath sign).

As you proceed, on your right, note the course of the High Peak Railway as it crosses a gully on an embankment.

[5] About one third of a mile from the road the trackway, just after passing a derelict yellow brick water works building, crosses a small bridge and starts to bend to the left. After the bridge branch off the

stone surfaced trackway onto the green trackway leading away to your right. Follow this green trackway as it runs to the south along the eastern side of Anthony Hill until it ends at a small quarry. From here keep on to the south between the hill on your left and the trackbed of the High Peak Railway on your right.

Soon the path comes up to the trackbed of the railway (where it is in a cutting) and then continues to the south alongside it.

When you get past Anthony Hill an impressive embankment comes into view to the south east. This, as has already been noted, is not part of the original High Peak Railway but was made in 1892 as part of the realignment programme carried out by the LNWR.

[6] After crossing a stream and going through a kissing gate you find yourself on Health and Safety Executive land with green and white banded posts marking the course of the path. A little way up the slope the path joins the trackbed of the High Peak Railway for a short way.

After just over 100 yards you come to a road crossing the trackbed of the railway with a notice indicating the way taken by the public footpath to Brandside. Here you are at the point where the original course of the High Peak Railway diverges to the south from the later 1892 realigned route. Over to the south east you should be able to make out the course of the original High Peak line returning to the north up the other side of the valley. You will get a better view of this section further on.

[7] Turn right and follow the road uphill to the south west. After passing to the left of a stone building, turn left onto the tarmac road that leads off to the south (signposted 'Public Footpath to Brandside via Dalehead').

At the point in the little valley beyond to the south where the tarmac road ends, a look to the left will reveal an embankment belonging to the original High Peak Railway.

Follow the posts uphill to the stile which gives you access to the Axe Head Moor to Earl Sterndale road.

[8] Turn left and proceed to the east along this road.

Just round the bend ahead you have on your left a good view of the original course of the High Peak Railway as it loops round and then heads straight to the north. On this straight stretch a long low tunnel like structure, erected in connection with the Safety in Mines Research Establishment, has been built on the track bed. To the north, beyond this, a sharp sided cutting through a limestone spur can be made out. This cutting is part of the 1892 work. The course of the original High Peak line went round the spur the cutting passes through. With binoculars you can spot some short stretches of steeply graded narrow gauge track (just above the 'long low tunnel') used in connection with the Safety in Mines Establishment.

From the bend continue on the road for three-quarters of a mile (ignore the turning to the right) until you come to the right-hand bend just beyond the racing circuit on the ground over to your left.

[9] Here climb over the wooden stile on your left and make your way to the north east, keeping to the right of the tumbled stone wall that runs straight up the hill ahead to the north east.

Near the highest point of the path a few paces over to your left you will be able to look down on the whole of the original course of the High Peak Railway on the wide loop later cut off by the 1892 deviation. Note at the bottom of the embankment nearest to you is what looks like the blocked entrance to a trackway tunnel passing through the embankment. From here too you get a better view of the narrow gauge railways of the Safety in Mines Research Establishment.

From here also, but over to the east, at one time you could have probably have made out most of the original course of the High Peak Railway as it twisted and turned following the contour as it made its way towards Parsley Hay. Sadly, later quarrying has almost completely obliterated this section of the original line but one part just east of Hindlow has been left undisturbed and can made out from where you are with the help of binoculars. Look at the north side of the furthest quarry working and you should be able to make out the course of this section of the High Peak Railway as it bends round the north side of the hill running between two stone walls.

From the highest point of the path continue on to the north east, keeping to the right of barbed wire fence which has appeared on your left (ignore the stile over this fence).

[10] At the neck to the west of Staker Hill go through the horse gate and

follow the new stone surfaced trackway downhill, keeping the new wooden fence on your left.

As you go down the courses of both the original High Peak Railway and the 1892 realignment come into view. The original line, with its partly stone revetted embankment and the one nearest to you, lies just below you. This section of the original line continued in use even after the new realignments were opened in order that Hillhead Quarry, round the hill to the south east, could continue to be served by rail.

Continue on along the trackway which bends a little to the right to cross the trackbed of the original line with its (later) wooden sleepers with chairs attached still in place. A little below, a gate and stile give access to the trackbed of the 1892 line.

In this view (near point 11) the original course of the Cromford and High Peak Railway is on the left and that of the later London and North Western Railway on the right.

[11] Go left on the trackbed of this line and follow it as it crosses an embankment making for Harpur Hill to the north west.

Beyond the embankment the 1892 line joins the course of the original

High Peak line. The two run as one for just over half a mile, passing the site of Harpur Hill goods depot (where a trackway crosses the railway) and a large disused limestone quarry on the left. Just beyond was the site of the Hoffman Lime kiln which was lit in 1875 and said to have burnt continuously for the next 70 years. Some stone work up against the rock wall on the left probably marks the site of this kiln which was served by a siding from the High Peak Railway.

Continue along the trackbed of the railway as it bends round to the south west.

[12] Soon after the buildings of the industrial estate beyond come into sight a well used footpath goes to the right off the railway trackbed. Follow this path as it goes to the north and then bends to the right to reach a short side road that goes to the north between some terraced houses to reach the Harpur Hill to Ladmanlow road.

[13] Turn left and go west along this road for almost three-quarters of a mile until, on your right, you come to a footpath notice pointing up the hill to the north (ignore the first footpath sign which is on the right just after the crossing of the stream).

Follow this footpath straight uphill, aiming for the stone tower called Solomon's Tower visible above.

[14] From the top of the tower on a clear day you have a superb view of the countryside round about including the course of the High Peak Railway. From the tower with binoculars you should be able to spot the entrance to Hindlow Tunnel (to the south east) on the later line which enabled the old line of the High Peak Railway, still partly visible on the hill above, to be abandoned in 1894.

From the tower take the well used path to the north west. Keep to the south of the boundary wall of Grin Wood. After passing through a little cutting you will find yourself back at the start of the walk above the picnic car park.

Walk 10: The Cromford and High Peak Railway: Hindlow to Sparklow

Map: Pathfinder Map 777 SK 06/16 or Outdoor Leisure Map 24 'The Peak District White Peak area'.

Distance: 12 miles including deviations or 8 miles omitting the deviations.

Start: The junction of the Chelmorton to Newhaven Road with the Flagg to Brierlow Bar Road at the south end of Chelmorton Village. Grid reference SK 110 695. (The alternative starting point for those who intend to shorten the walk by walking one mile along the A515 is at the picnic car park on the High Peak Way at Sparklow. Grid reference SK 128 659. From here the walk can be picked up at point 12 and followed to point 14 from where you can proceed west along the A515 for just over a mile and then pick up the walk again at point 4.)

By Car: Chelmorton is about 4 miles south east of Buxton and about 1 mile on the north side of the A515 Buxton - Ashbourne Road from which it is well signposted. Roadside parking is available in Chelmorton Village to the north.

By Public Transport: Buses run from Buxton to Ashbourne on the A515. The walk can be picked up at point 4 by alighting at Sterndale Moor opposite the ICI quarry at Hindlow.

This walk follows the Cromford and High Peak Railway in an area which, though much disturbed by recent quarrying, retains much of interest and much of its beauty. The view from the ridge above Earl Sterndale is particularly fine. Easy going underfoot and no steep climbs.

The suggested walk begins well away from the course of the High Peak Railway so that the exploration of its remains can continue from west to east and also so that a round walk can be made, avoiding any long lengths along the busy A515 Buxton to Newhaven Road.

The Railway

The section of the High Peak Railway followed on this walk covers about four-and-a-half miles stretching from east of Hindlow to Parsley Hay. This section consists of the last part of the level section east of the top of Bunsall Incline to the top of Hurdlow Incline, Hurdlow Incline itself and the start of the level section running from the bottom of that incline to the top of Hopton Incline about 17 miles away.

Hurdlow Incline had the shortest life of all the eight original inclines on the High Peak Railway. In 1855 an Act authorised a single line deviation on a gradient of 1 in 60 thus allowing Hurdlow Incline with its gradient of 1 in 16 to be closed and enabling locomotives to work through from the top of Bunsall Incline to the top of Hopton Incline. The opening of the new route by the LNWR enabled the section between Dowlow and Harpur Hill to be abandoned in 1892. A short section of the original route at Dowlow, though widened and otherwise brought up-to-date continued in use and, indeed, remains in use today to enable rail borne traffic to come out of Dowlow Quarry, thus making it the only section of the original High Peak Railway to remain open for traffic.

Despite extensive recent quarrying in the area hereabouts, most of the earthworks of the original route on the section which this walk covers remain in a remarkably good state of preservation.

The Walk

[1] Cross over the stile in the wall on the south side of the road to Brierlow Bar a few yards west of the junction (footpath sign). Go diagonally across the field to the gap stile in the south west corner. Go diagonally across the next field, aiming for the stile in the south west corner at the end of a line of trees (ignore the stile in the south east corner of the same field).

[2] Cross the little dry valley ahead and then turn slightly right, aiming for the metal gate to the south west through which a farm track runs. Once through the gateway continue to the south west, aiming for the stile between the two gateways in the wall ahead. Once over this stile go diagonally across the next field, aiming for its south-west corner, just over the brow in the middle of the field.

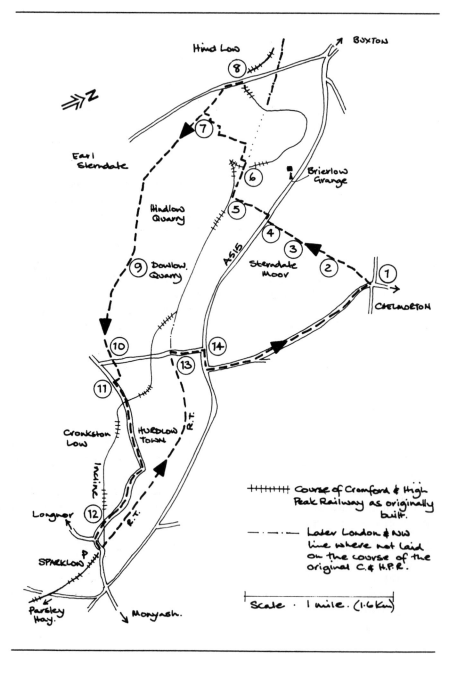

⇒Z

Hind Low

⑧

BUXTON

Earl
Sterndale

⑦

Brierlow
Grange

⑥

Hindlow
Quarry

⑤

④

③

Sterndale
Moor

②

①

A.515

CHELMORTON

⑨ Dowlow
Quarry

⑩

⑬

⑭

⑪

Cronkston
Low

HURDLOW
TOWN

R.T.

Incline

Longnor ⑫

R.T.

P

SPARKLOW

Parsley
Hay.

Monyash.

++++++++ Course of Cromford & High
Peak Railway as originally
built.

—..—..— Later London & NW
line where not laid
on the course of the
original C.& H.P.R.

Scale · 1 mile. (1·6 Km)

[3] Once over the brow a stile (just to the right of the houses ahead) becomes visible. Also now visible over to the west is the course of the High Peak Railway as it comes round the north side of Brierlow Hill and runs to the south east behind a long thin plantation of trees after which it runs on an embankment which, with its opening for a farm track to go through, is easily spotted.

Go over the stile and make your way along the west side of the rough playing field.

[4] At the south west corner the path emerges onto the Buxton to Ashbourne Road between two houses. Cross over (taking care) and go through the gap in the wall opposite (signposted 'Public Footpath to Longnor'). Follow the path through a thin strip of woodland and then along the west side of the long field which follows to the south.

[5] When you come to the present day railway, turn sharp right across the metal bar stile, and then proceed to the west, keeping immediately north of the railway boundary wall.

[6] At the end of the field another stile gives you access to the trackbed of the High Peak Railway. From here you can see the course of the railway approaching from the north in a cutting through the limestone hillside and then running on an embankment to where you are standing. It then crosses over the later railway and bends round to the east running on a low embankment to join the course of the present railway just before the stone road bridge of later railway date.

To the south of where you are standing, on the other side of the present day railway, the outlines of a reversing triangle on the High Peak Railway can be made out. This reversing triangle was probably provided so that wagons, having come up the inclines on one side of the summit level, could be turned before going down the inclines on the other side of the summit level. The wagons, it is believed, needed to be turned because they had end doors which always needed to be at the upper end when the wagons were on an incline. Alternatively, or as well, some wagons may have had doors on one side only and needed to be turned to suit certain platforms and goods sheds.

Another point here: as the High Peak Railway's original line continued in use right up to the opening of the new line through Hindlow Tunnel in 1892 the old line must have been carried across the cutting of the new line on some sort of temporary structure.

Make your way a few yards west to the bridge carrying the farm track over the present railway. Cross over and then immediately turn right. Follow the path as it makes its way to the south west via a series of right-angled bends, keeping to the west side of the next three fields. The route is well signposted and stiled. The stile in the south west corner of the last field gives you access to a wide track running north west to south east along the edge above Earl Sterndale.

[7] From this point a diversion of a quarter of a mile will reveal a short length of High Peak Railway trackbed, not yet destroyed by quarrying, of the section which once ran on the north side of Hind Low. Those making the diversion should turn right after crossing the stile and proceed north west along the ridge track until the Brierlow Bar to Earl Sterndale road is reached.

[8] About 150 yards northwards along this road on its west side (opposite the south end of a line of trees on the east side of the road) the course of the High Peak Railway can be seen bending away to the north

The vast cavity created by the workings at Hindlow Quarry contrast vividly with the gentle limestone hills. View looking North West, North of point 9 of the walk.

west on an embankment having, presumably, crossed the road by a stone bridge. Barely 150 yards further on the course of the line has been obscured by quarry earthworks. Back now to the point where the ridge track was joined.

From the stile where the track was joined (turning left after coming over the stile if the diversion has not been followed) follow the track as it runs to the south east along the ridge for one-and-a-quarter miles. On the left are vast cavities made by Hindlow and Dowlow Quarries while, in complete contrast, on the right there is a superb view over the upper part of the Dove Valley with North Staffordshire beyond. Take care to use the shelters provided if the blasting whistle sounds.

[9] Where the track ends go over the wood stile in the wall in the left-hand corner and not through the gate at the end of the lane. Keep on in a south easterly direction with the stone field wall on your right. Two stiles and 500 yards further on you come to a field with its boundary wall on your left leading away to the north east. Do not follow this wall but aim for the stile (between two yellow posts) in the field wall opposite about 50 yards to the south of the north east corner of the field.

[10] Cross the stile, turn left in the green lane you find yourself in and go north for about 50 yards until you reach the brow of the hill.

From here you can see the course of the High Peak Railway moving away from the course of the later line and crossing your lane on the level about 300 yards further down the hill from where you are standing. You will get a closer look at this section of the High Peak Railway on the return part of the walk. Return to the point where you joined the green lane.

Go through the gap in the wall on the east side of the lane (way marked in yellow) opposite the stile you came over. Go to the east north east, keeping to the left of the stone wall running in the same direction for about 250 yards until a wall coming from the north blocks the way. Here turn sharp right through the gate and make your way southwards across the field to the stile in the wall opposite. Cross over this stile onto the Earl Sterndale to Hurdlow Town road.

[11] From this point you have a good view of one of the best preserved sections of the central part of the High Peak railway as it bends to the

east crossing over on a stone embankment pierced with an opening for a farm track and then running along the north side of Cronkston Low to the top of Hurdlow Incline. Go eastwards along the road towards the hamlet called Hurdlow Town.

After 150 yards you come to the point where the High Peak Railway crossed the road on the level. The cutting to the north has been partly filled in but can still easily be made out. On the south side of the road, amongst a tumbled pile of stones, at the time of writing, was a stone sleeper with a single drilled hole.

Continue eastwards along the road through Hurdlow Town hamlet.

East of the hamlet, where the road bends to the south, you have a good view of the earthworks of Hurdlow Incline going downhill at a gradient of 1 in 16. Leaving the top, the 850 yard long incline railway ran first on a high embankment and then on the surface of the slope itself. The incline was the longest of the original separately worked inclines on the High Peak Railway, lowering the railway some 160 feet down the hillside.

[12] The course of the incline crosses the road you are on just north west of the hamlet of Sparklow (posts bearing electricity wires run on the trackbed) and then continues in a straight line downhill to disappear in the earthworks of the later railway just north west of the road bridge over that railway.

Where the road joins the Longnor to Monyash road turn left. After a few yards leave the road to take the path on your left that drops down to the High Peak Trail which runs here on the course of the original High Peak Railway though all the bridges and earthworks are of later LNWR work.

A worthwhile diversion or extension of the walk (or an idea for a walk at another time) is to follow the High Peak Trail as far as Parsley Hay two miles away to the south east. While for the most part the later LNWR trackbed, on which the trail runs, follows the course of the original High Peak Railway, there are parts where the two diverge. The first of these is at the first bend to the south east where the later line smoothed out the sharper bend of the original line.

A quarter of a mile further on, where the trail on the later line crosses the Endmoor to Pilsbury road in a straight line and obliquely, on the west side of the road at least, one can make out the remains of the original High Peak Railway as it approaches the road at an angle nearer to a right-angle than that of the later line.

Just over a quarter of a mile south of this road crossing the course of the older line diverges to the south to run round the spur of the hillside, while that of the later line curves gently through the spur in a cutting. To the east of this cutting the course of the older railway crosses the course of the later railway and then runs to the east on the side of the slope before bending to the south east to rejoin the course of the later line which has cut across this section on an embankment.

About 350 yards further on the later line has slightly cut out the sharpness of the original bend in the older line. Just under half a mile further on Parsley Hay is reached where there is another easing out of a bend.

Back at Sparklow make your way to the north west, following the High Peak Trail. This part of the Trail is on the course of the deviation authorised in 1855 but opened only in 1869 as a single line. The bridges and earthworks are, however, for double line and therefore belong to the work of doubling completed in 1894.

[13] After just under three-quarters of a mile the Trail ends at the same unmetalled lane crossed earlier in the walk further to the south. A diversion of just over 200 yards to the south along the lane will bring you to the point where the High Peak Railway crossed over on the level. A cutting can be seen to the west while to the east an embankment succeeded by a cutting can also be seen. The embankment, it will be noted, looks wide enough for one track only.

[14] Make your way to the north on the lane to its junction with the main road from Buxton to Ashbourne. Here turn right and make your way to the east for 200 yards along the main road. Then, taking care, cross over and go along the much quieter road to Chelmorton. After just over a mile this road will bring you back to the start of the walk.

This is the last of the four walks exploring the fascinating remains of this early railway. If all the High Peak line were to be covered by walks like these a whole book would be needed for this one railway itself. Fortunately, however, unlike the sections covered so far, the section east of Parsley Hay is opened to the public for its entire length and also, unlike much of the central section with its realignments, remains very much as it was when the railway was opened in 1830. It is certainly worth walking on or cycling on for its entire length right down to the terminus of the eastern end on the Cromford canal. Also the Middleton Incline engine house with its engine still in working order is not to be missed. It will give you a good idea of what was once to be seen at the top of the inclines these walks have explored.

Walk 11: The Caldon Low Railways (i)

Map: Pathfinder Map 810 SK 04/14

Distance: 7 miles

Start: The picnic car park at Froghall Wharf three miles north of Cheadle. Grid reference SK 027 476.

By Car: The picnic car park is situated on the lane to Foxt which branches north off the A52 Stoke-on-Trent to Ashbourne road about 300 yards north east of Froghall Bridge in the Churnet Valley just beyond the junction with the road to Ipstones. If coming from the north you should turn right off the A 523 Stockport and Macclesfield to Ashbourne road onto the road to Ipstones (the B5053) at the junction about 4 miles south east of Leek. At the T junction 1 $^1/_2$ miles south of Ipstones turn left onto the A 52. The lane to Foxt follows on the left after just a few yards. The picnic car park is 200 yards further along the lane.

By Public Transport: The Potteries Motor Traction bus services 234 and 236 Leek to Cheadle and Tean pass through Froghall. The service is, however, not very frequent.

The two walks along these railways (Walk 11 and Walk 12) explore the considerable remains of four early railways which in succession linked the limestone heights at Caldon Low to the depths of the Churnet Valley at Froghall. Both walks take the railway explorer through much varied and pleasant landscape on the north side of the Churnet Valley. On the first walk the only steep climbs are up the former railway inclines while on the second walk there is a fairly steep climb up the old lane to Foxt. Otherwise the going is not too strenuous, though in winter and after wet spells parts can be very muddy underfoot.

The Railways

There cannot be many examples of two places linked by no less than four railways built in succession within a space of just over 70 years and all on different alignments, while one of the places, Caldon Low, has had, and indeed still has, yet another railway linking it to the outside world. For the sake of convenience and for quick reference on the walks the four railways or tramways linking Froghall to Caldon Low will be referred to as Railways 1, 2, 3 and 4 respectively.

Railway 1

The story of this early railway goes back to the 1770s when proposals were made for a branch canal to link the Trent and Mersey Canal to the limestone quarries at Caldon Low in the north east part of Staffordshire. One early proposal, described, in fact, by Josiah Wedgwood of pottery fame, envisaged a canal running via Leek to the western side of Caldon Low, involving tub boats being raised up by inclined planes instead of by locks. This scheme was not, however, proceeded with and instead a canal was built from the Trent and Mersey Canal at Etruria up the Churnet Valley as far as Froghall. The canal appears to have been opened for use from the end of 1778.

At the same time as the canal was being dug a railway or tramway was under construction from the original canal basin (just over 500 yards west of the present basin and by the road to Ipstones) up the valley of the Shirley Brook and over Shirley Common to the limestone quarries at Caldon Low some 1,100 feet above sea-level. As the canal basin was at 430 feet above sea-level, the railway had to climb some 670 feet in just three-and-a-half miles in order to reach its destination. The railway, which presumably opened at the same time as the canal, was laid with track which consisted of flat cast iron rails spiked down upon wooden sleepers. It is possible that John Gilbert, agent to the Duke of Bridgewater and a partner in some collieries in Shropshire served by an early rail system, may have been responsible for laying out the line. The course of this first railway has been traced up the Shirley Brook as far as the point where it runs towards Shirley House Farm. Beyond here its route is uncertain.

This first railway was not well laid out and was recognised even by contemporaries as being unsatisfactory. It was said to be 'very crooked, steep, and uneven in its degrees of declivity in different parts'. In frosty weather wagons slid so much that the carrying of any worthwhile amount of limestone became impossible. You can imagine the problems of the wagon men trying to calm and control their terrified horses (horse-power was the sole motive power on this line) in these conditions. It was decided, therefore, to rebuild the railway on what was virtually a new alignment.

Railway 2

The Act for the second railway up to Caldon Low was obtained in 1783 and included provision for a 530 yard extension of the canal to what is now the canal basin at Froghall. From this new basin the railway climbed steadily, hugging the eastern side of the valley of the Shirley Brook (Railway 1 kept to the bottom of the valley) to just beyond Harston Brook where it turned to the south to run up the side of a tributary valley. Once out of the tributary valley the line ran over Whiston Common and on past Garston House, climbing gently up the hillside until it passed over the crest of the ridge separating the valley of the Churnet from that of the River Hamps to the north, ending at the quarries at Caldon Low just over half a mile beyond.

The track was of the same type as was used on the first railway and again horses provided the tractive power. Each horse was able to make three journeys a day on at least four days during the week bringing down one wagon at a time. By 1790 the new railway was already giving problems and £834 had to be spent on improvements. Before long this second railway was found to be inadequate to cope with the increasing demand for limestone from Caldon Low so, only 19 years after the Act for its opening was passed, the canal company decided to replace it with an entirely new railway which, apart from the section at the terminal ends, was again on a new alignment.

Railway 3

This third railway or tramroad was built under the provisions of an Act passed in 1802 with John Rennie as its engineer. It was probably completed before the end of 1803. Unlike its two predecessors which were worked entirely by horse-power, Railway 3 used horses as motive power only on the relatively level sections between four self-acting inclines. One could therefore say that gravity provided the main motive power on this line which a contemporary observer, John Farey, described as being amongst 'the most complete works of this kind in Britain'. The track, which was double, consisted of lengths of flanged plates spiked to stone blocks so, of course, the wheels of the wagons would be flangeless as on the contemporary Peak Forest Tramway.

From Froghall Wharf, where sidings led to ten 'Tipplin-machines' from which the limestone was discharged into the canal boats, the line ran to the bottom of the first incline a few yards away. This 65 yard long incline had at the top a large horizontal drum, round which a chain was wound. Descending wagons, loaded with limestone and attached to this chain, would draw up by the force of their weight ascending wagons which were either empty or lightly loaded with coal. From the top of this incline sidings ran to the top of the lime kilns, while other tracks ran to the bottom of a second and much longer incline barely 60 yards away.

This photograph illustrates the activity at Froghall Basin as the final railway from Caldon Low disgorges from its wagons limestone ready for transhipment to the canal barges. *Reproduced by kind permission from The Manifold Collection.*

This next incline, known as the Great Froghall Plane, was 303 yards long and was equipped with an endless chain which passed round two wooden pulley wheels turning on vertical axis and housed under a large open shed at the top of the incline. Where the chain dragged between the rails on the plane itself, cast iron saddle shaped blocks were fixed in order to guide it. Wagons went up and down the incline in trains of five at a time, their speed being controlled by a brake on the pulley wheels.

From the top of the Great Froghall Plane there was a level run of about three-quarters of a mile to the bottom of the third incline known as Whiston Plane. This incline, situated at the east end of the village of Whiston, was 150 yards long and was worked in a similar way to the Great Froghall Plane.

From the top of the Whiston Plane Rennie's tramroad proceeded, with a slight rise, for one mile to the bottom of the fourth and final incline, namely, the 294 yard long Upper Cotton Plane which was worked in the same way as the Great Froghall Plane. The approach to the bottom of this incline was made in a deep cutting. This expensive piece of earth moving was done in order that there should be a uniform gradient on the incline. The same effect was achieved at the Whiston Plane by placing the approach to the top on a long high embankment. From the top of the Upper Cotton Plane a nearly level run of three-quarters of a mile, which included a cutting through the ridge at the top of the valley, brought the line to its destination at the quarries at Caldon Low.

The wagons used on Rennie's plateway or tramroad were basically wooden with sides sloping outwards at the narrow ends. Iron hoops were fitted to the wagons to take the shock when they inevitably banged together on the inclines. On the 'level' sections of the line a horse could draw 12 loaded wagons on the downward run and take 12 empty wagons back up though extra horses were needed on some sections, at least, if the returning wagons were loaded with coal.

Rennie's plateway or tramroad lasted 47 years, which was somewhat longer than its two predecessors. Like its predecessors, however, it too was in turn replaced by a new railway on yet another alignment in order to increase the amount of limestone that could be brought down in a day.

Railway 4

The final railway to be made between Froghall and Caldon Low was built in 1849 by the North Staffordshire Railway Company who had acquired the Trent and Mersey Canal Company and hence the canal at Froghall in 1846. The new line, apart from bends at the terminal ends, ran in a straight line between the canal basin and the quarry. Basically, the railway consisted of three roughly one mile long inclines directly following each other with, therefore, no level sections of any length in between. These self-acting, cable-operated inclines had wagons going up and down in trains of up to nine wagons at a time, enabling up to 1,000 tons of limestone per day to be transported. This was a considerable improvement on the 250-270 tons per day capacity of its predecessor. The earthworks connected with this new line were considerable and included a well made tunnel of almost 400 yards length. The track was laid to the gauge of three feet six inches.

Shunting of wagons at both ends of the line was done with horses, though after 1877 locomotives took over much of the work at Caldon Low end. The two locomotives providing this service were 0-4-0 saddle tank engines named 'Toad' and 'Frog' and supplied by Henry Hughes of Loughborough. In 1901 they were joined by a Bagnall built locomotive called 'Bobs'.

In 1905 yet another railway was opened to Caldon Low. This was the standard gauge line from Leekbrook Junction near Leek. The new line approached Caldon Low from the north west. For the time being the North Staffordshire Railway Company kept both lines open but it was not long before the cost of transhipping at Froghall and the costs of working the inclines began to tell against the older railway. On 25 March 1920 the narrow gauge line to Froghall officially closed thus bringing the story of almost a century and a half of rail borne transport between Caldon Low and Froghall to an end.

The outward part of Walk 11 follows as closely as possible the course of Rennie's tramroad (Railway 3) of which the impressive earthworks remain substantially intact. The return part of the walk follows closely the virtually undisturbed trackbed and earthworks of the narrow gauge inclined railway (Railway 4). En route you will come across much of the remains of the middle and upper sections of the 1783 railway – (Railway 2).

The Walk

[1] Froghall picnic place itself is situated on the very site of the start of the later three of the four railways running up to Caldon Low. No doubt sidings from Railways 2 and 3 would have criss-crossed the site, while Railway 4 had sidings all over the place, including some which crossed over to serve the area on the west side of Foxt Road which now bisects the present picnic site.

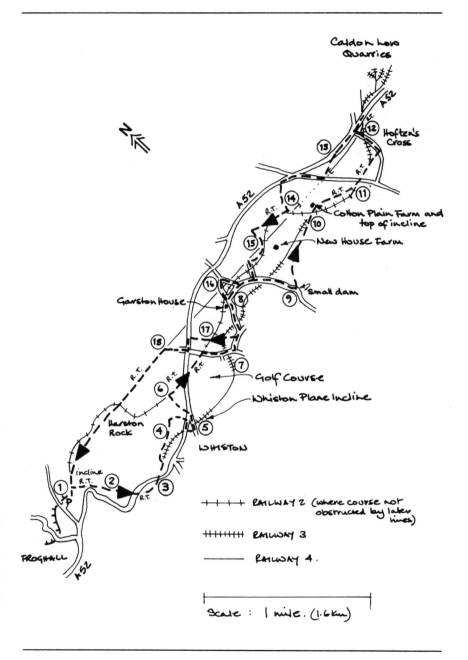

Make your way to the north east end of the picnic site and walk up the slope in the corner. This slope is, in fact, the earthwork of the short first incline of Railway 3 and known as the First Froghall Plane. The incline was also utilised by Railway 4 thus giving it an active life of over 115 years.

At the top note the massive stone footing of the horizontal winding drum which controlled the ascent and descent of the wagons. Not all the wagons loaded with limestone arriving from Caldon Low went down this incline. Some went off to both left and right to have their contents tipped into the lime kilns bordering the north and east side of the canal basin. The kilns to the left of the incline top are the older of the two sets.

Make your way across the flat area at the top of the incline to the house opposite, at the side of which is a signpost reading 'Public Footpath to Whiston'. Further on to the north east the second incline of Railway 4 led off in a cutting but this is not for now as this will be covered on the return walk. Proceed to the south east up the footpath to Whiston which goes between two stone outbuildings to the left of the house. The northernmost of the two outbuildings is, in fact, situated on the site of the bottom of the second incline of Railway 3 and known as the Great Froghall Plane. Once past the outbuildings the course of the incline running straight up the hillside become clear. Make your way uphill on the incline trackbed.

Where the incline rises on an embankment to cross a lane you have to go off to your left as the stone arched bridge, which once carried the railway over the lane, has gone. Remount the incline on the other side of the lane.

[2] At the top of the inclined plane the path goes through the archway between the two houses built on what must have been the site of the mechanism containing the two pulley wheels round which the continuous chain for raising and lowering the wagons wound. Just past the houses note the small older stone building on your left. This may possibly have been a stable for some of the horses working the level section as far as the bottom of the third incline. Continue south eastwards along the trackbed of this level section which here is used as a road to get to the houses you have just passed.

In just under 400 yards you come to the point where Railway 3 crossed the Whiston to Froghall road (now the A52) on the level. Cross over and go through the foot gap in the wall opposite. The right of way continues on the course of Railway 3 as it bends gradually round to the east until once again it crosses the road on the level but this time at more of an oblique angle.

[3] Go along the path to the left of the Methodist Chapel opposite and continue eastwards on the trackbed for about 100 yards until you come to a foot gap in the wall on your left. As the right of way here leaves the trackbed of Railway 3, go through the foot gap and then turn right.

The trackbed of Railway 3, as it winds its way among the trees, makes a pleasant walk between points 2 and 3.

Follow the wall on your right until you come to another foot gap (don't be misled into following the well used path that goes diagonally across the field). Pass through and keep straight on with the wall on your right until halfway before the next crossing wall you come to a foot gap in the wall on your right. Pass through and turn left to continue roughly in the same direction as before but now with the wall on your left.

The trackbed of Railway 3 is not far below you on your right and is marked by a row of large hawthorns, while ahead of you the remains of the third incline of Railway 3 can be seen rising sharply up the hillside to the east. This was known as the Whiston Plane.

[4] Go through the foot gap at the side of the gate ahead and then bear a little to the left to pass through a wide gap (no gate), aiming for the foot gap visible to the north east just to the left of the brick farm building. Go through, turn right and pass through the farmyard to pick up the lane that leads off to the south east to link up with the A52 road. Turn right at the main road and go to the south west for just over 100 yards until you come to the gate at the start of the second field on your right.

Here the course of Railway 3 coming from the west crosses the main road on the level to pass to the bottom of the third incline a few yards on the other side. Cross over the road and go through the foot gap opposite. The path follows the railway trackbed for the few yards to the bottom of the inclined plane and then bears to the right to climb up to the lane which crossed over the railway on a stone bridge. This bridge is intact but, unfortunately, filled in underneath.

[5] Once up on the lane turn left onto the bridge itself. Above you, to the east, the upper part of the remains of the Whiston Plane rises steeply on a high embankment which, despite some cutting into, is still largely intact. Now continue on to the north east along the lane until you come once more to A52 road.

Cross over the main road and go through the foot gap on the opposite side of the road. Go diagonally across the field you find yourself in, aiming for the foot gap (not visible at first) in the north corner of the field and well to the left of the red houses ahead. Go through and proceed northwards, keeping the wall on your left (ignore the stile over it).

[6] At the north end of the field you come to a gate on your left. Through this gate once ran Railway 2 after a long steady climb from the canal basin. This section of Railway 2 is covered in walk 12 from its start to point 5 of that walk

Turn right and go eastwards following the faint traces of the trackbed of Railway 2 as it runs along the north side of the field. Away to your right you have a good view of the high embankment leading up to the top of the Whiston Inclined Plane of Railway 3. This is a rare feature for, while inclines themselves often run on embankments to smooth out their gradients, it is rare for the incline top itself to be on an embankment with an embankment running up to it on the level section.

At the end of the field cross over the A52 road and continue on in the same direction on the footpath opposite (wooden post footpath sign). This continues on the course of Railway 2, though it is not obvious here.

After about 300 yards the footpath ends at a lane. Beyond the lane the course of Railway 2 continues eastwards on the west side of the stone wall running in the same direction but, unfortunately, there is no right of way on it from here onwards. Turn right on the lane and make your way to the south east to pick up the course of Railway 3 again.

[7] About 250 yards further on, a hump in the lane marks the point where Railway 3 crossed on the level. On the left a grass covered storage tank has been placed on the trackbed. Proceed on and at the junction less than 100 yards further on go left to take the lane leading off to the north east.

On your left from the lane, at the far end of the first field, the course of Railway 3 can be seen bending to the east to enter a shallow cutting before going under the lane further on, while Railway 2's trackbed can be made out in the middle of the field beyond making for the north side of Garston House. Just after the lane bends to the left, and just to the south of the white house beyond, Railway 3 passed under the lane by a bridge the east side of which still seems to be intact, though mostly buried. Continue along the lane to the north east.

[8] At the next junction go right. The slightly raised trackbed of Railway 3 is visible on your right at it bends round with the contour, while over on your left the course of Railway 2 can just be made out in the first field.

Go right again at the next junction and follow the lane as it goes downhill to the south east. Soon another white house is passed. Less than 100 yards further on Railway 3 crossed the lane on the level and then bent slightly to the left to pass immediately north of the old barn visible in the field to the east.

[9] About 350 yards further down the lane, at the start of the major bend to the right and by small dam a little way to the left, a farm road goes

off on the left-hand side. Immediately at the start of this farm road on the north side is a foot gap. Lift up the sheet of tin with the handle on and go through. Go northwards through the next foot gap ahead and then make for the foot gap in the corner of the field below the garden wall of the house ahead. Go through, turn left and make your way north eastwards, passing the farmhouse on your left.

Aim for the point where the wall to the north meets the stream (ignore the foot gap in the north west corner of the field). Once there go through the gate, cross the stream and then keep on to the north east aiming for the bottom of the large mound of spoil ahead.

As you proceed, over to the left, the course of Railway 3 can be seen where an embankment crosses the stream higher up. After this the railway entered a deep cutting, the spoil from which formed the mound you are making for.

Go round the south side of the mound. At the east end you can look down into the cutting out of the east end of which rose the fourth and final incline of Railway 3 known as the Cotton Plane. Cross over the stile ahead and make your way uphill on the incline trackbed. Note the piece of limestone with grooves worn in it by the rope or chain (it looks more like rope wear) lowering and raising the wagons on the incline.

[10] About halfway up the incline, on your left, the course of Railway 4 running on an embankment can be easily made out. More difficult to make out is the course of Railway 2 which approaches from the north west, having crossed the course of the later Railway 4 between the end of its embankment and the start of the cutting which follows. It next passes underneath the earthworks of the incline of Railway 3 which you are on and then goes south eastwards gently climbing up the side of the ridge.

At the incline top the trackbed, as is usual on an incline plane, suddenly levels off and you find yourself next to Cotton Plain (could it have once been Cotton Plane?) Farm. Don't go through the foot gap on your left which gives access to the farm road but continue along the course of Railway 3 as it bends to the right away from the incline top to run south east immediately south of the hedge running in the same direction.

After about 150 yards you come to a wide gap in the north east corner of the field you are in. On your right, not far below, the course of

Railway 2 can be seen bending round the slope and passing through a gateway as it climbs up nearer to the course of Railway 3 which you are on.

Continue straight on but now to the north of the hedge. About 150 yards further on you pass through another gap and the hedge is on your left again. On your right the course of Railway 2 can be seen coming up to join that of Railway 3. Both then enter the cutting on the left, though it is possible that the cutting belongs to Railway 3 only and that Railway 2 climbed over the rise the cutting goes through, though following the same course.

[11] Go through the gate to the right of the start of the cutting and then turn left to follow the tarmac track which goes eastwards between a house and the cutting until you come to a public road. Railway 3 (and Railway 2?) crossed under the road just to the left but, unfortunately, the bridge has gone.

Go over the stile opposite and continue following the course of Railway 3 (and probably Railway 2) as it runs to the east. After just over 200 yards the cutting ends and the course of the railway starts to bend to the left. Here a stile gives you access to some waste ground at the back of some new houses. Go round to the left of the low building ahead and make your way between the houses up to the road ahead and then turn left.

[12] Follow the road northwards for about 150 yards. Just opposite the north end of the older type terraced houses on your left, go right off the road onto the track which bears off slightly to the right off the road. This trackway is on the trackbed of Railway 3 and probably that of Railway 2 and perhaps that of Railway 1 (see introduction) as well.

Go over the stile and proceed north eastwards. The remains of Railway 4 can be seen coming in on the left on an embankment to join the course of the other railways. So for the first time since leaving Froghall it is likely that the course of all three railways correspond. If the possibility of Railway 1 is added, it could be said that no less than four different railways or tramways at different times passed over this spot.

Another stile gives you access to the A52 road. Ahead lies Caldon Quarry, the destination of all four lines. Unfortunately, later quarrying has destroyed the remains of the railways beyond here. The first edition

Ordnance Survey map indicates that Railway 3 ran just to the left of the village hall ahead and then split into several short branches to serve the quarry face which was not far beyond.

Now for the return walk which follows closely the route of the last of the four railways, namely, Railway 4 and also gives some further glimpses of the remains of Railway 2.

Make your way westwards along the A52 road for just over quarter of a mile. On your left Railway 4 ran on an embankment and then entered a deep cutting before running through a tunnel.

[13] Leave the main road where it bends slightly to the right and a farm road goes off to the left. The path has no proper gate or stile at this end so make your way over the one strand of barbed wire that runs on the west side of the farm road. Next make your way to the west south west diagonally across the field, aiming for the side of the far end of the cutting of Railway 4. Unfortunately, even in winter, undergrowth obscures the view of the tunnel entrance at the end of the cutting.

Having passed round the end of the cutting, keep straight on to the foot gap through the wire fence and stone wall ahead. Once through, turn right on the road and proceed north westwards as far as the junction with A52 road. Here turn left and follow the A52 road for just under 200 yards until, opposite the first house on your right, you come to stile low down below the road on your left. Climb over and go straight down the field in a south westerly direction.

[14] At the brow of the hill you have a good view both of the clear straight course of Railway 4 running westwards on an embankment after leaving the tunnel and of the less obvious course of Railway 2 bending round, roughly following the contour, to the north of Railway 4's embankment. Make an 45 degree turn to your left and drop down the hillside, aiming for the foot gap in the stone wall bordering the trackbed of Railway 4.

Having examined the trackbed, make your way to the north west, following the tumbled stone wall going away from the former railway's boundary wall in the same direction. After about 100 yards, at the point where another tumbled wall comes down the hillside to join the tumbled wall you are following, the trackbed of Railway 2 can just be made out coming up to join the path you are on from the left.

At the next wall coming down on your right a foot gap gives access to a large field. From here the trackbed of Railway 2 can just be made out as it bends gently away to the left, following a stone wall until it crosses the course of Railway 4. There is no right of way on this section of Railway 2 so keep straight on in a north westerly direction across the field until you come to a cement farm road. Turn left on this road and follow it southwards.

[15] The road crosses over the trackbed of Railway 4 on a stone bridge. Also at this point the course of Railway 2 crosses over that of Railway 4 and then proceeds to the south west, gradually bending to the right.

Just south of the bridge turn right off the road through the wide metal gates at the south end of the first field on your right. Go on in a westerly direction, keeping the field wall on your left. Note the faint signs of the trackbed of Railway 2 coming in on your right.

Go through the wide gap and proceed on westwards, but now with the wall on your right, to pass to the north of the ruined house ahead. Just past the house go through the foot gap on your right and make your way diagonally across the field to the gate in the north west corner. Through the gate you find yourself on a narrow green lane with a bridge over the course of Railway 4 on your right.

Having looked over the bridge, make your way south westwards down the green lane. Railway 2 crossed the lane on the level at the bottom of the field with the ruined house in it. The trackbed, although not much raised, is not too difficult to make out on either side of the lane. Continue on to the bottom of the lane and then turn right on the tarmac road.

Proceed west along the road, keeping right at the Y-junction. Railway 2 ran just behind the farm on the right and, having crossed the road on the level just above the Y-junction, continued westwards towards Garston House. Next along the road you cross the course of Railway 4 running in a sharp side cutting.

[16] Go left at the junction of the tarmac lanes just beyond and soon once again Railway 4's course is crossed.

About 50 yards beyond this latter crossing, Railway 2's course is crossed once more. It can be seen coming across the field on your left to pass immediately north of Garston House which is the first house on your right. Continue south westwards, keeping right and passing once again over the course of Railway 3 (crossed over on the walk out) until the road bends to the right.

Go through the gate on your right, just past the bend, turn left and make your way to the next field to the west, walking parallel to the road. Go through the gate into this field and then turn right. Proceed to the north west, keeping the wall on your right until you come to the stile in the north corner of the field (it is not visible until you are almost at the corner). Railway 3 ran immediately to the south of the curving wall marking the north boundary of the field.

Cross the stile, then keep on to the north west, crossing the wooden stile in the fence ahead and making your way to the corner of the stonewall jutting out a head. Don't miss the stile which is just to the left of the corner - do not continue to the north west in the same field. The course of Railway 2 can be seen coming from the side of Garston House to the east and making its way to the west, to Whiston Common on the north side of the wall through which the stile passes. The Whiston Common (now a golf course) section was covered on the outward part of the walk. Now to pick up Railway 4 again.

[17] Once over the stile continue to the north west with the stone wall and later the hedge on your right. Two stiles more and you find yourself back on the A52 road again. A 150 yard diversion to the right brings you to yet another bridge over the trackbed of Railway 4 as it continues to the west and downhill in an almost straight line. The current edition of the Ordnance Survey map shows a right of way on the trackbed west of this point but, unfortunately, there is no obvious way down and the trackbed is overgrown so it is best to make your way back down the A52 to where you joined it.

About 100 yards further along the A52 road beyond the stile you came over, a farm road goes off to the right. Go along this farm road until it starts to climb up to a bridge to take it over the course of Railway 4. Here go off to the left onto the track that leads onto the trackbed of the railway below the bridge and then proceed along the trackbed to the west.

[18] Soon you find yourself at the top of the almost one mile long incline which took Railway 4 down to the top of the final short incline above Froghall Basin. There are several tantalising mounds with fallen

stones and bricks scattered around but nothing to indicate clearly the working at the top of the incline. Make your way to the west following the trackbed of the incline.

After a cutting, a high but somewhat eroded embankment follows. At the west end of the embankment Railway 2 once ran underneath. This section of Railway 2 is covered in more detail on Walk 12.

Continue westwards along Railway 4's incline. Cuttings interspersed with sections terraced out on the valley side follow. Finally, a long cutting with a gentle bend (the first on this railway since Caldon Low) brings you to the area above Froghall Basin and the picnic car park where the walk began.

Walk 12: The Caldon Low Railways (ii)

Map: Pathfinder Map 810 SK 04/14

Distance: 3 miles

Start: The picnic car park at Froghall Wharf three miles north of Cheadle.

By Car: The car park is situated on the lane to Foxt which branches north off the A52 Stoke-on-Trent to Ashbourne Road 300 yards north east of Froghall Bridge in the Churnet Valley.

Transport: The Potteries Motor Traction bus services 234 and 236 Leek to Cheadle and Tean pass through Froghall. The service is, however, not very frequent.

This short incline above Froghall Basin was used by both the third and fourth railways from Froghall to Caldon Low. *Reproduced by kind permission from The Manifold Collection.*

126

The outward part of this walk follows as closely as possible the fairly intact remains of Railway 2, while the return journey picks up the more scanty remains of Railway 1.

The Railways

These are described in the introduction to Walk 11.

The Walk

[1] Make your way to the north east end of the picnic site and proceed up the slope in the corner. This slope belongs, as those who have already done the previous walk will know, to Railways 3 and 4. Railway 2 probably rose to the rim of the canal basin on a gentle gradient on a course now buried under the earthworks of the two later railways.

At the top make your way north east on the flat area between the two houses to where the trackbed of the next incline of Railway 4 begins. The private road branching off to the left at this point probably follows the course of Railway 2. Unfortunately, however, there is no right of way over this road so one must proceed by going up the footpath on the trackbed of Railway 4's incline which begins its climb in a cutting with a gentle bend in it.

[2] After about 200 yards a footpath branches off to the left. A few steps diversion onto this path will reveal the course of Railway 2 as it begins its long climb out of the valley of the Shirley Brook. Basically the course of the Railway 2 for just under the next half a mile is parallel to and just to the north of but below that of Railway 4. Unlike the latter, however, which runs in a straight line after the bend at the bottom, Railway 2's course twists and bends as it clings to the side of the valley, involving, in some places, substantial earth and stone works where terracing out from the side was necessary. The trackbed is easily made out, at least in winter when there is no foliage on the trees.

Now go back to the main path and continue on uphill to the east on the later railway's trackbed.

[3] Stop at the first of the short sections of wooden protective fencing which jut out from the left into the course of the path. From here the course of Railway 2 can be seen coming from the west, bending round

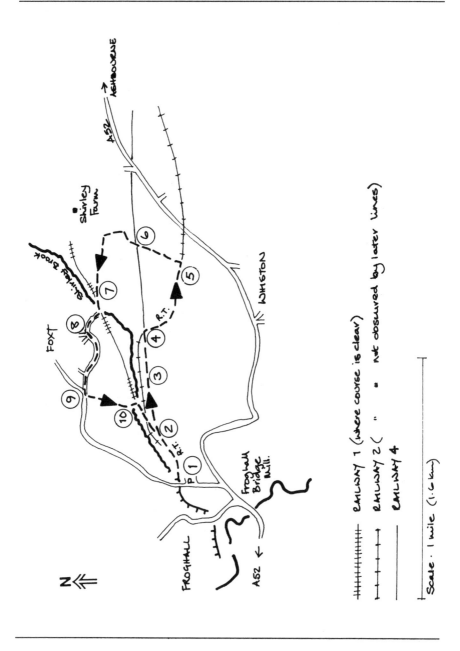

the hillside to run just underneath the earthworks of the later railway on whose trackbed you are standing. The older railway was here terraced out above the valley below on a stone revetted bank. Beyond, to the east, its course moves away from under that of the later railway to bend round the spur on the slope of the valley, while Railway 4's course goes straight on.

Continue on the path until you come to the next jutting out protection fence. Here Railway 2's course can be seen again but this time a little further down on the slope than at the last stop.

[4] Continue on along the main path through the cutting until you come to the point where Railway 4 crossed the deep sided valley on a substantial embankment. Here, on the west side of the side valley, the course of Railway 2 can be made out coming in on the left, passing underneath the trackbed of Railway 4 and then going off to the south east clinging to the side of the side valley.

Do not cross the embankment but go to your right off the trackbed of Railway 4 to drop down onto the trackbed of Railway 2 and follow it as it winds away to the south east. Note the older railway's embankment with its valley side stone revetted. This and the previous stone work indicates that this early railway was no lightweight affair. After a cutting, the course of Railway 2 bends round to the left. Here the trackbed has been disturbed by slippage and spillage of loose ground. The path following the course of the railway is, however, still easy to follow.

[5] Where the wood ends go over the stile next to a gate and continue straight on in an easterly direction, keeping the hedge on your left. The path here is still following the course of Railway 2, though the trackbed is not as clear as before in the wood.

A gap next to a second gate follows. Again keep straight on but now with the hedge on your right. Stop when you get to the next gate.

Here, for the first time in over a mile, the railway levels off for a considerable distance. You can imagine the relief to both horse (or horses) and human leader when reaching this point after a long pull with the 'empties' from the canal basin below. Here too this walk leaves the course of Railway 2 (the rest of its remains as far as Caldon Low are covered on Walk 11) to go to the north east to pick up the remains of an even earlier railway to link the canal to the quarries at Caldon Low, namely, Railway 1.

In front of the gate turn left and go uphill to the north east, keeping the hedge on your right. Just over the top of the hill be careful not to go through the gate where the hedge ends and a wall begins. Instead keep straight on, still with the wall on your right, until you reach the stile in the north east corner of the field.

[6] Once over the stile, cross straight over the narrow area of disturbed ground which is, in fact, the remains of the top of one of the inclines of Railway 4 linking the canal to Caldon Low (see Walk 11). Go over the stile in the far corner opposite. It needs a little looking for as it is hidden by a corner in the wall.

Go downhill to the north east, passing to the right of the massive rock ahead. Go through the foot gap below, cross the farm road and follow the wall beyond, keeping it on your left, as it bends round to the north. Go through the gap next to the metal gate and continue following the wall as it bends round to the left to run now in a westerly direction. After passing through another gate you find that the wall bends away further to the left. Keep straight on here to drop down the slope to the north west corner of the field above the trees filling the bottom part of the valley of the Shirley Brook.

[7] Here at the bottom of the field the wide trackbed of Railway 1 can be seen running up as a clearly defined terrace just above the line of the trees. It ran on in a north easterly direction until it turned somewhere, probably near Shirley Farm, to make for Shirley Common but of this part and beyond there is no clear trace.

Cross over the stile in the corner of the field and follow the trackbed of Railway 1 as it goes to the south west. After about 50 yards you come to the remains of an embankment with a large round arched stone culvert which carried the railway over the Shirley Brook. The culvert is partly collapsed but enough is intact to enable walkers to safely cross the brook on it. Note the use of good quality ashlared stone to make up the side and arch of the culvert.

A few yards further on the path and the railway trackbed make a junction with the old lane from Foxt to Garston. The railway, having crossed the lane on the level, continued on near the valley bottom to the south west. Unfortunately, there is no right of way on the railway trackbed from here onwards so turn right, go over the stile and follow the green lane uphill for about 200 yards.

Near point 7 on the walk this well built large stone culvert pierces the embankment which once carried the first railway between Froghall and Caldon Low.

[8] Just past some old sheds on the left, the lane widens and starts to bend to the left. Here go over the stile on your left and follow another old lane that bends round the hillside roughly on the contour to the west. As you proceed, on your left, you have a dramatic view over the valley of the Shirley Brook. Well down below, the course of Railway 1 can be picked out running along the north side of a rough wooden fence and then a stone wall.

[9] The old lane after winding round the hillside joins a tarmac road. Go left, follow the tarmac road for just under 100 yards and then turn left down the side road leading to a group of terraced houses below. Where the side road ends keep straight on downhill, passing over a stile, until you come to the bottom of the valley once more. Near the bottom make your way to the left of the clump of birch trees that lie ahead.

[10] Near the brook the trackbed of Railway 1 can be seen approaching from the east as a broad flat levelled way dropping gently down the slope above the brook. It, and the path you are on, cross the Shirley Brook on a culverted embankment similar to the one met with further up the river, except that this one has an extra small arch beside the main arch. West of the crossing, the course of the railway is far less clear though it appears to have run close to south side of the brook.

Continue westwards on the well used path through the woods. After about 250 yards a left-hand turn soon brings you back to the main path on the trackbed of Railway 4 walked on the outward journey. Turn right and you will soon find yourself back at the start of the walk.

Walk 13: The Scout Moor Quarries Tramway

Map: Pathfinder maps 690 SK82/92, 700 SD 61/71 and 701 SD 82/92

Distance: $4^1/_2$ miles.

Start: The roundabout on the A56 (T) at the southern end of the Edenfield by-pass in Rossendale. Grid reference SD 795 185.

By Car: If approaching from the south leave the M66 at junction 1 (signposted Ramsbottom) and turn onto the A 56. After just over 2 $^1/_4$ miles follow the A56 road off to the left (signposted Burnley). The round-about where the walk begins follows after $^3/_4$ mile. There is a large lay-by suitable for parking immediately south west of the round-about on the left of the start of the road to Stubbins.

By Public Transport: Frequent bus service from Bury. Soon trains from Bury could be stopping once more at Stubbins Station, just $^1/_3$ of a mile to the west.

This walk takes you quite quickly from the urbanised Irwell Valley into the comparative loneliness of the upper reaches of the Dearden Valley. The walk outwards follows closely the course of the tramway as it climbs up the south side of the Dearden Valley. The return section runs along the lip of the north side of the same valley giving some fine views as well as a good overall view of the former tramway. The route involves some steady climbing up to 1,300 feet (about 400 metres) above sea-level so avoid days when there is very low cloud covering the moors. Some parts of the walk can be quite wet underfoot, especially near the upper end of the tramway where wet mossy bog has spilled over onto the trackbed.

The Railway

This tramway, for so this railway is called on Ordnance Survey maps, was of three foot gauge. It was opened in 1880 in order to bring stone from the Scout Moor Quarries down to a terminus on the Edenfield to

Rochdale Road where the stone was transferred onto road vehicles. The line was owned by James Whittaker and Son who were also agents for Aveling and Porter and so, not unnaturally, their first locomotive was built by this firm. This was a 2-2-0 well tank which looked more like a traction engine than a railway engine and was given the name 'Excelsior'. This engine was replaced round about 1912 by a more normal looking narrow gauge locomotive. This was an 0-4-0 saddle tank built by W.G. Bagnall in 1904 and appropriately named 'Scout Moor'. This engine had previously worked at Walshaw Dean where it was named 'Esau' (cf. Walk 1).

In order to reach the quarries situated high up on the hillside but only about half a mile from the Edenfield Rochdale road terminus, the tramway had to proceed one-and-a-quarter miles up the Dearden Valley with a climb of about 200 feet to a point where it reversed and then climbed about another 100 feet in the reverse direction to reach its destination.

This 'Scout Moor' was used by the reservoir contractors using the Scout Moor Tramway. The photograph was probably taken between points 7 and 8 of the walk. *Reproduced by kind permission from The Haslingden Library.*

In 1905 the tramway was extended from the reversal point to the site of a reservoir being built for the Bury and District Water Board half a mile further up the valley. The reservoir traffic was worked by a Peckett 0-4-0 saddle tank locomotive also apparently named 'Scout Moor' with a second locomotive called 'Cray' (it had once worked at the Cray Waterworks of the Swansea Corporation) which was an 0-4-0 wing tank. As the navvies lived at Scout Fold near Turn village there may well have been a 'Paddy Mail' service to convey them to and from the works site.

The reservoir was officially opened in October 1909. On the day of the opening the members of the Water Board travelled on à special train nicknamed the 'Scout Moor Express'. Problems with leakage caused work on the reservoir to continue long after the official opening ceremony and it was not until 1912 that the work was finally completed. After this the reservoir branch of the tramway would have become disused, though for some reason, as will be seen on the walk, it was never completely dismantled.

This view of the Scout Moor Tramway illustrates well how work usually proceeded at a stone quarry face in the Rossendale Hills. *Reproduced by kind permission from The Rawtenstall Library.*

The main line of the tramway came to an unexpected end when in about 1939 an extensive landslip, approximately three-quarters of a mile from the lower terminus, carried a large section of the trackbed, complete with sleepers and rails, over a 100 feet down the hillside. That the closure was not planned is shown by the fact that 'Scout Moor' (the first one) was left in the engine shed with a new cylinder lying alongside waiting to be fitted. It was not until 1962 that this locomotive was cut up on site, the Aveling Porter locomotive having been removed the year before to Aveling Barford's works at Grantham for preservation.

The Walk

[1] Go up to the east on the A56 from the roundabout until you come to a T-junction. Here turn right. After about 100 yards turn left up a trackway that leads off eastwards between a bungalow and a semi-detached house.

[2] This is Hollins Lane and is signposted as a public footpath. The lane after bending left and then right, makes a T-junction with Bury Old Road which is now only a rough lane. Here turn left and make your way northwards along the road until you come to its junction with the A680 Edenfield to Rochdale road. Cross over, turn right and make your way up the road to the south east until you pass the last of the first set of terraced houses on your left with a new detached house beyond.

[3] The Scout Moor Quarries tramway had its shed and workshops on the mound which you can see on your left. Landscaping has, unfortunately, recently destroyed the track formation here except for a short length of embankment leading away to the north east from behind the next row of terraced houses up the road.

Continue along the road for about a 100 yards until you come to the end of a third row of terraced houses. Here take the road on your left (footpath sign) leading straight up the hillside to the east.

As you proceed, you may be able to spot on the hillside ahead, a little to the right of the last quarry dump, the remains of an incline on which coal was once brought down from Scout Moor Colliery to the village of Turn below.

[4] After passing a farm on the left, the road becomes brick surfaced.

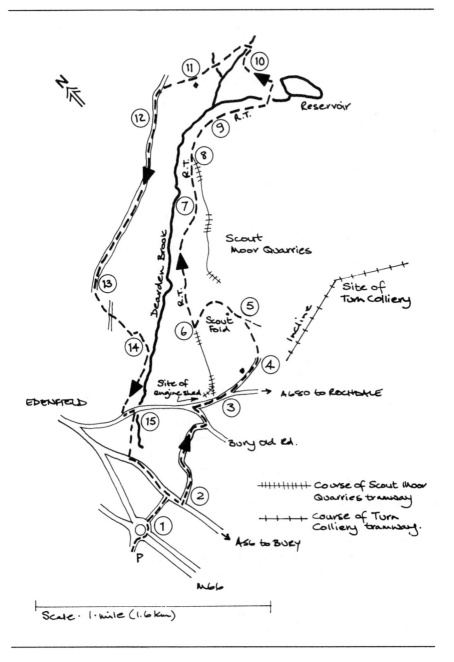

Follow this road as it bends gently to the north east until it bends sharp right. Here, going left off the brick road, make your way onto the unmetalled trackway leading off northwards.

If you look down to the left you should be able to make out the course of the Scout Moor tramway as it bends away to the north east from between the two rows of terraced houses and passes through a stone wall east of Cote Farm House. A wire fence marks its course for a while after this gap.

[5] Continue along the trackway until you come to a fork roughly level with the last of the scanty remains of Scout Fold. Take the lesser used trackway on your left here. Walk along it keeping the wire fence on your left until, as the trackway fades out, the wire fence ends and a good stone wall bends off to the left downhill. Follow this stone wall downhill (keeping it on your left) until, at the bottom of the steep slope, it bends somewhat to the right.

[6] At this point there is a gate. It was through this gate that the tramway once ran. Turn right and follow the course of the tramway (on which the right of way now runs) as it continues its steady climb north eastwards up the side of the Dearden Valley. At first the trackbed is filled with rushes but soon conditions underfoot improve and a few sleepers can be spotted.

An embankment follows next. Presumably the slope of the hillside was too unstable here for terracing to take the tramway. Next the trackbed bends slightly to the right and the upper part of the valley comes into view. Then suddenly the tramway appears to end. Ahead is only a jumbled mass of ground. Here you are at the spot where the extensive landslip of 1939 brought the tramway operation to a sudden end. Well down the slope on your left a number of wooden railway sleepers can be seen. One set is still in its original position on the trackbed which now lies well away from its pre-1939 position.

Continue straight on, making your way across the disturbed ground until on the far side you pick up the trackbed once again, still in its original position. Continue on along the trackbed.

[7] Not far along you will notice on your right a short but steeply graded siding, with sleepers still in position, leading up to the ruins of some stone buildings. What were they for?

Continue following the 'main line' as it carries on climbing up the side of the valley. Despite some minor landslips, the trackbed is basically well-preserved here. In less than a quarter of a mile you come to the main reversal point (look for the trackbed coming in on your right).

[8] Here, where the 'main line' changed direction, the whole train would reverse and then proceed up the steep climb on the right to reach the quarries just beyond the top of the climb. At the bottom of the reversal section wooden sleepers are still in their original positions and clearly indicate the exact course of the tramway, though further on, in the quarry itself, the course has been somewhat obscured by later workings. This reversal point, as stated in the introduction, was for many years the furthest point east reached by the tramway. In 1905, however, the line was extended further up the valley to the east in order to serve the works connected with the building of a new reservoir. It is along this section that the walk proceeds. Although filled with rushes in certain sections, the trackbed is easy to follow.

Although high up in the hills, the Scout Moor tramway still had a long way to climb to reach the quarry whose tips dominate the horizon on the right of the photograph.

After a sharp curve to get round a gully, some rails may be noted still in their original positions. The next feature to note, on your right, is a small platform made of sleepers. Possibly this had something to do with the small mine with its two, now blocked, levels just above.

Continue on along the trackbed of the tramway as it begins to bend to the east and then to the south east as it continues climbing up the valley.

[9] Where the tramway trackbed passes through a gap in a stone wall the official right of way leaves the trackbed, drops down sharply to cross the stream below and then climbs straight up the other side of the valley, to the left of the collapsed stone wall up to the brow. However, because this route is very steep it is suggested that you do as most walkers do, namely, continue along the trackbed to where it ends at the bottom of the reservoir. Go down the bank to your left here, cross the stream and then make your way up the other side, keeping to the left of the reservoir boundary wall until you come to a hard surfaced trackway leading away from the reservoir to the north. Follow the trackway as it goes to the north and then to the north east, close to the lip of the valley. The official right of way comes up on the left and joins the trackway here.

[10] Continue on the trackway until it makes a sharp bend to the right away from the brow of the hill. Here go straight on over the rough pasture and over a tumbled wall, keeping on the lip of the clough which is on your left. Just before you come to a second stone wall you will meet, at right-angles, a path running parallel to this wall. If you look carefully you should be able to spot some stone slabs used for paving the path. Turn left and follow this path as it crosses the stream and then turns to the north west, gradually dropping down to a ruin in the distance.

[11] Pass the ruin, keeping it on your left. Now make for a gap in the tumbled wall across the path a little above the junction with the wall that runs up to it from the ruin. When you get there you will see that the gap is, in fact, the remains of an old stile. Continue straight on, climbing gently until, just past a second ruin, you come to a hard surfaced trackway. Turn left and follow the trackway westwards as it drops down in the direction of Edenfield.

[12] As you proceed you will have an excellent overall view of the Scout

Moor Quarries tramway, including the reversal up into the north end of the quarries. From the top of the north end of the Scout Moor Quarries you may notice what looks like a former railway running from a second reversal to a mine tip roughly above the start of the first reversal. Although partly covered by later quarry tipping, it looks convincingly like a branch of the tramway. It isn't, however, but is just a well made stone surfaced track, leading southwards from the mine and presumably disused by the time the quarries came into use.

[13] The hard surfaced trackway eventually disappears into a yard next to a water board house. Bear right here and go along the boundary fence for a few yards. At the first gate turn left and go downhill in a southerly direction, keeping the wood with its boundary wall on your left. Follow the path as further down it crosses over the water board road and keeps straight on going now through the wood. At the end of the wood cross over the wooden stile and turn left on the rough lane (part of the old road to Bury).

[14] Follow the lane until you come to a footbridge. Don't cross the bridge. Instead keep straight on the trackway which runs along the north side of the Dearden Brook. The track becomes a road and brings you onto the Edenfield to Rochdale road. Cross over and go left for a few yards. Then turn right onto the path (footpath signpost) that goes through the mill yard on the south west side of the road. This path will bring you onto the Edenfield to Bury road where a left turn and then a first right turn will bring you back to the start of the walk.

Walk 14: The Tramways of the Grane Valley

Map:Pathfinder Map 689 SD 62/72

Distance: just under 4 miles.

Start: The junction of Grane Road (Haslingden - Blackburn B6232) and Holcombe Road (B6235) at Holden. Grid reference SD 774 225.

By Car: Approaching from the south after leaving the M66 you will find yourself on the dual carriageway A56 road to Burnley. Follow the A56 where it diverges to the left from the road to Rawtenstall keeping on it till you come to the B6232 (Darwen and Blackburn South) turn off. Here go left. The start of the walk is about $1/3$ mile further on. At the junction where the walk begins Grane Church (spire) is on the south west side and the Holden Arms on the south east side. On the north side by the cemetry the road is wide enough for parking.

By Public Transport: A regular bus service (Rawtenstall - Haslingden - Helmshore Circular) goes along Holcombe Road.

This walk over the hills flanking the lovely Grane Valley in the west of Rossendale explores the considerable remains of one quite lengthy quarry railway system and glimpses the remains of a second system. The walk is mainly on field paths and involves two moderate climbs.

The Railways

The first railway or tramway this walk will come across is that which serviced Grane Quarry situated high up on Musbury Heights, just above the 1,000 foot contour. The three foot gauge tramway started at a wharf adjacent to Grane Road Sidings on the former Lancashire and Yorkshire Railway's Bury to Accrington line about one mile south of the site of Haslingden Station. From here the line wound its way up the Grane Valley, past Holden Wood Reservoir, to the bottom of a long incline situated just under a mile from the start of the line. The incline, almost certainly self-acting, led directly up to the quarry where there was a quite extensive tramway system.

As is often the case with Rossendale quarry lines, dates are difficult to come by. An Ordnance Survey map of 1891 shows the tramway and also shows that quarry had been extensively worked by that time so a date of opening round about 1875 seems reasonable.

Not much is known about the engines that worked on this system. The engine that worked from the wharf to the incline was called 'Roscoe' apparently after one of the quarry owners. Another engine, either unnamed or with its name unremembered, is known to have worked in the quarry itself. Between about 1903 and 1910 the lower part of the system was used to bring materials for use in the construction of Ogden Reservoir for the Bury and Radcliffe Waterworks. The contractors, at first Foster and then Phineas Drake, used several locomotives for the reservoir work. Among these were locomotives named Ogden, Hannah and Crookfoot, the latter being locally called 'Croo Toot'.

The only recorded accident on the system occurred in 1906 when an employee of the Grane Quarry Company, after falling 'while shunting', was run over by a railway wagon loaded with stone, which took off both his legs below the knees. The poor man, who was in his 50s, 'succumbed to his injuries' that same night.

The date of closure is uncertain but the tramway is still shown on a map of 1928 survey. Much remains of the Grane Quarry tramway, despite the unfortunate obliteration of the bottom of the incline by some waterworks buildings. Some reworking of quarry material started in 1987 but was fortunately stopped before much damage was done.

Of the three foot gauge tramway that once served Hutch Bank Quarry on the north side of the Grane Valley, because of later quarrying, not much remains. The tramway consisted of an internal quarry system with an incline, almost certainly self-acting, which led directly down from the lip of the quarry to a wharf situated just above Grane Road. Although the wharf was not far from the Lancashire and Yorkshire Railway's Grane Road Sidings, from what one can make out from contemporary maps, it would seem to have interchanged traffic with road vehicles only.

The quarry was in operation in 1871 and is still in operation today, hence the destruction of much of the remains of the quarry tramway

'Hannah' was one of the engines which was used on the lower section of the Grane Quarry Tramway by the contractors building Ogden Reservoir. *Reproduced by kind permission from The Haslingden Library.*

system. The quarry belonged for many years to Brooks and Brooks who also owned the series of quarries served by the tramway system above Cloughfold (see Walk 15). At least one steam locomotive is known to have worked in the quarry itself. This was an 0-4-0 saddle tank called 'Ant'. 'Ant' is believed to have been made in Gatehead in 1861 and to have served in several locations before coming to Rossendale in 1878. It could well be identical with the 'Ant' that served the other Brooks and Brooks three foot tramway, namely, that above Cloughfold east of Rawtenstall. This 'Ant', anyway, is believed to have been at Hutch Bank in the 1890s and was certainly scrapped there in 1924. 'Ant' was said to have been able to haul six wagons which compared well with the maximum of two wagons which its diesel successor could haul.

The tramway is still shown on a map of 1928 survey but most likely closed soon afterwards.

The Walk

[1] Go along the track which starts from the junction of the 'B' roads opposite the Holden Arms immediately to the left of the private car park south of Grane Church. The track is signposted 'Public Footpath to Holden Reservoir'. Halfway towards the reservoir a look left will reveal the first section of the Grane Quarry tramway. The tramway began at an exchange wharf which was situated away to the east just to the right of the large yellow building which houses the Snow King frozen food depot. The sidings of the exchange wharf are now covered with wooden garages but the trackbed of the tramway, as it starts off towards where you are now, can readily be made out with the high revetted stone bank supporting it on its south side. The tramway then bent to the south to pass under Holcombe Road below you, emerging in a cutting immediately beyond the stone wall to the east of where you are. Nearer the reservoir, if you look back, you will see that this cutting still retains its stone revetting on one side.

[2] Proceed on to the north end of the reservoir embankment. It was here that the tramway crossed over your track on the level, though here it has left little trace.

Continue on the track as it crosses over the retaining embankment of Holden Wood Reservoir (completed 1841) and then bends round to the west to run along the slope on the south side of the reservoir. As you go along this section over on your right you will have a good view of the course of the tramway as it weaves its way along the north side of the reservoir immediately south of the reservoir boundary wall. Ahead to the west the incline leading up to the quarry from the west end of the reservoir soon comes into view.

[3] Keep on the trackway until, after passing through two gateways, you see a large wooden stile over the fence on your left. Cross over the stile and follow the marker posts to another large wooden stile up at the south west corner of the field. Cross over this stile and also a third similar stile just a few yards away over the fence on the south side of the next field. Now make your way along the path that runs uphill in a westerly direction immediately to the right of a wire fence and a tumbled wall.

[4] At the top you will find yourself passing just below the hump at the

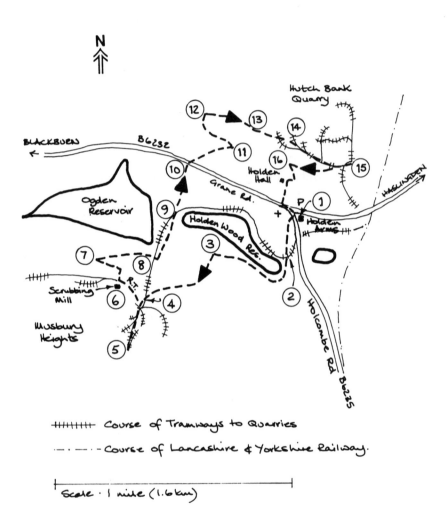

+++++++ Course of Tramways to Quarries

—.—.—.- Course of Lancashire & Yorkshire Railway.

Scale · 1 mile (1.6 km)

top of the incline of the tramway, while to your right is a deep cutting through which the track of the incline passed. An examination of the top of the incline will reveal the remains of the brakes man's hut and the pit for holding the bottom of the frame containing what was locally called the balancing wheel. The timbers which held its vertical axle are still there but fast rotting away.

Beyond you will see some damage to the original tramway layout caused by some recent stone recovery work which fortunately stopped before things went too far. Make your way past the new mound south of the incline top to a large flat space behind. Here the tramway wagons would have been shunted before being lowered down the incline. You can imagine what a hive of activity this place would have been with a little steam engine busily shunting wagons around and then puffing away with a train of empties on one of the branches that led away to the west, south and east. The remains of the branch to the south are well preserved and worth exploring.

Proceed along the tracked of this southern branch as it bends away from the west of the shunting space through a cutting in a tip of waste or overburden. Even before it has completed the bend to the south the remains of a another branch leading off to the left can be seen. Continue on past the Rossendale Way sign ('RW') on a large stone to the left of the main branch. The course of the main (south) branch threads its way through tips. Along the way after a branch going off to the right, you come to a trailing junction on the left.

[5] The main branch ends by a deep pit on your left situated just in front of the southern boundary wall of the quarry. Often in Rossendale quarries the quarrymen would follow a good section of stone downwards thus creating some very deep pits. At the side of each pit a stone platform for a crane would be built. The platform for the crane of this pit can be clearly seen. While here it is worth going right up to the boundary wall to appreciate the view over the valley of the Musbury Brook with Tor Hill beyond.

Retrace your steps back to the shunting space by the incline head.

Once back there make your way to the west, along the trackbed of the west branch of tramway from the incline head. As you go along, you may notice a few wooden tramway sleepers decaying away still in their original positions.

[6] After about 200 yards you come to the remains of the scrubbing or polishing mill. The gaunt remains of its chimney, unfortunately badly damaged by lightning and half collapsed in the winter of 1983/84, tower above. The course of a short branch, probably to carry coal for the boiler, can be seen leading to the south side of the mill. Note the loading platform made of large blocks near the north side of the mill.

You may wish to explore the rest of the trackbed of the western branch right to the end of the quarry. Its course is well preserved with many wooden sleepers still in place but please note that, although people freely wander along it, there is no right of way on this section.

From the scrubbing mill take the footpath (the Rossendale Way) that leads across the mounds to the north. When you come to a point where you have an open view across the valley the path turns left. After a few yards a marker points you straight downhill. After a few more yards the path bends to the left to drop gently down the slope to the west.

[7] Continue on the path until, just a few yards from the start of a wire fence on your left, you come to a stream. Don't cross the stream but turn sharp right onto the path in front of it which drops down the slope in an easterly direction.

After going downhill for about 250 yards the path emerges onto a wide flat terrace. This could well have been the site of the puddle field for the Ogden Reservoir (built 1903/10) below. When you come level with the retaining embankment of the reservoir you will be able to pick out the distinct remains of a double incline leading down from the terrace to the reservoir below.

[8] A few yards further east you will find yourself in front of the embankment carrying the lower part of the Grane Quarry tramway incline. Notice the little foot tunnel for past users of the way you are on to pass under the incline in safety though now you are best advised to go over the incline. On the other side of the embankment go through the white gate ahead a few yards away and turn left. Make your way down the field to the north, keeping the wire fence and then the iron fence of the waterworks on your left. At the bottom cross the stile and go over the footbridge.

Immediately north of the footbridge the tramway crossed the path and then bent round to the south to reach the foot of the incline.

Unfortunately, because of later waterworks development, no trace of the tramway remains at that point.

[9] Go through the gap between the stone wall and the wire fence ahead and make your way diagonally across the long field you find yourself in, making for the gate at its far north end. It is not easy to see from the bottom of the field so aim for the middle one of the three stone houses ahead, i.e. the unpainted house facing south with a south facing gable on its right.

[10] On reaching the gate go through and cross over the road. Next go up the farm road opposite leading away in a north easterly direction (public footpath signpost). At the end continue straight on through the farmyard. The footpath goes on a flagged way immediately to the right of the little garden wall in front of the farmhouse on your left. At the end of the flagged way go through the half-size gate on your left. You will now find yourself in a large field. Go across it in a north easterly direction, aiming for a little gate in the north east corner of the field.

High up on Musbury Heights the half-collapsed chimney of Grane Quarry scrubbing mill points its gaunt finger skyward. The main line of the tramway ran to the right.

[11] Go through this gate onto the farm road and turn left. Follow the road as it winds its way uphill to the north west. On the way up if you look across the valley to your left you will have an excellent view of the full length of Grane Quarry and its incline. Also worth noting are the tramway links associated with the work in connection with the construction of Ogden Reservoir. There is not only the incline at the west end of the likely puddle field but also, further away to the west, a third incline. This ran from a quarry about half-way up the hillside down to the reservoir. The bottom part is obscured by the by-wash channel but as this would have been built towards the end of the works it still seems safe to assume that this third incline was also associated with the reservoir works.

[12] Continue along the road as it goes over the brow of the hill to its end at a stone house. Here turn right and go to the east, keeping to the right of the tumbled stone wall that runs to the east from a point level with the south end of the garden wall of the house. After about 100 yards cross over the stile and then keep straight on eastwards but this time keeping to the left of wire fence running in the same direction.

As you go along, you may notice the remains of what was perhaps a small coal pit. The width of the track leading away from it indicates that it was served by road carts rather than by railed vehicles.

[13] At the east end of the field go over the stile on your right. In front of you is a deep stone pit which was the furthest working to the west of Hutch Bank Quarry. The Ordnance Survey map of 1891 shows the Hutch Bank Quarry tramway serving the upper part of the western end of the quarry but, unfortunately, modern infilling has obliterated any trace of it here. What could, perhaps, be mistaken for a tramway trackbed at the bottom is, in fact, the surface of a road which once served this part of the quarry.

Go round the stone wall on your left and resume walking in a westerly direction. After a few yards the wall ends and a wire fence moves away from it to the left. Do not follow this fence but walk straight on, keeping on the top of the quarry infill. Hopefully it will be grassed over before you come to walk on it. At about the point where the new tipping ends there is a wooden stile just below the drop on your left. Cross over and go right on the track.

[14] Over on your right the Ordnance Survey map of 1891 survey shows the tramway running next to the road. Careful looking will reveal some traces. The wire fence is at first in the middle of its trackbed and then immediately to the north of it. At the point where the track dips down the tramway turned to the left to cross the track on the level at an oblique angle. Later quarry tipping on the left has obscured the course of the tramway beyond here.

Continue east along the track for about another 150 yards.

[15] At the point where the track bends round to the left and in front of a tip of large stones on your right you can see clearly the remains of the top of Hutch Bank Quarry incline, namely, a hump on a stone revetted embankment. Unfortunately, the site of the brakes man's hut and the sidings behind are now covered by later tipping. At least it preserves it for some archaeologist to uncover in some future century. The incline ran straight downhill past the west side of the farm below after which it bent to the east to cross the field below the farm diagonally to finish just behind the east end of the last row of terraced houses on the north side of the Grane Road. A 25 inch Ordnance Survey map shows the track on the incline as double from the top as far as the farm and then single to the bottom; a rather unusual arrangement.

From where you are standing you will also have a good view of the eastern terminus of the Grane Quarry tramway with its stone revetted embankment leading up to it.

Reverse direction and make your way to the west, keeping to the right of the fence running west from the incline top and aiming for the wooden stile situated a little below the trackway you have just left. Cross the stile and continue west, following an old deep hollow way. Go through the gate ahead and keep to the hollow way as it drops gently down the slope until it meets a stone wall at the bottom where it makes a junction with another old trackway.

[16] Here turn sharp left and follow this track (also a hollow way) to the south east. Pass the barn on your left and then turn right. After a few paces turn left and make your way southwards through the yard of Holden Hall Farm, keeping the house on your right. Follow the farm road southwards until you come to Grane Road where a left turn will bring you back to the start of the walk.

Walk 15: The Brooks Quarries Lines - Cloughfold to Blackhill

Map:Pathfinder Map 690 SD 82/92

Distance: about 4 miles.

Start: Junction of Hill End Lane and Peel Street with Bacup Road (A681) in Cloughfold in Rossendale. Grid reference SD 822 225.

By Car: From the south make for Rawtenstall which is easily reached by the A56 and A682 roads which are dual carriageway extensions to the M66 from its north end. From Rawtenstall go eastwards on the A681 Bacup Road. The junction where the walk begins is on this road about $1/2$ mile east of Rawtenstall town centre just past the Ashworth Arms and Woodfield Engineering works. The road name plates at the junction are not clearly sited so look out for the wooden finger post direction sign on the south side of Bacup Road pointing the way to 'Quarry Trail'. There is room for roadside parking on the north side of Bacup Road.

By Public Transport: Frequent bus service along Bacup Road from Rawtenstall and Bacup. By summer of 1990 a train service at weekends should be available to Rawtenstall from Bury.

Two walks are suggested to cover the exploration of the remains of this remarkable narrow gauge system, though they can be combined into one if it is so desired.

Walk 15 involves a steep climb followed by some rough moorland paths and tracks. The walk is interesting and worthwhile not only from the railway enthusiast's point of view, but also, because of its scenery, for the general walker. It offers a quick change from the terraced houses and mills of the valley bottom to the loneliness and openness of the higher moors of the Forest of Rossendale. On a clear day the walk gives views of far off hills both to the north and to the south so make sure you pick the right day to get the best out of the walk.

The Railway

The three foot gauge railway system serving the Brooks Quarries was the most extensive and one of the most interesting of the several railways in the Rossendale Hills. The system, which was owned by Butterworth and Brooks and later Brooks and Brooks, served no less than five completely separate quarries. It started at some standard gauge railway sidings immediately east of Cloughfold Station on the Ramsbottom - Bacup Branch of the Lancashire and Yorkshire Railway. From here the line went straight uphill on a steep and long incline. At the top of the incline branches went off to the east and the west to serve nearby quarries, while the 'main line' launched off southwards, climbing steeply, at least for adhesive traction, to reach the main quarry on the line, Cragg Quarry, a climb of some 400 feet, in just under two miles as the crow flies. Cragg Quarry was not, however, the final destination of the line, for an extension on two connected inclines over the watershed at 1,550 feet above sea level went on to Ding Quarry on the Rochdale side of Hail Storm Hill. This gave a 'main line' of about four miles but the system with all its branches, has been estimated to have covered some 11 miles.

Unfortunately, no photographs are known to have survived of this remarkable railway, despite the visit of rambling clubs, etc., to the system. Firm facts are also difficult to come by. The date of opening is unknown but the incline at Cloughfold was certainly in existence in 1867 when a certain Robert Dawson was killed on the tramway. He was struck by a loaded wagon while oiling the rollers over which the wire rope passed. In the same year a man was injured, while riding in the last of three wagons being drawn up the incline. The incline was of the self-acting type controlled by a wire rope passing round a balance wheel or drum at the top. There were several accidents on the incline, the worst of which was in 1888 when three loaded wagons broke free on the incline and, after hurtling down at break neck speed, crashed over into the public road at the bottom, snapping off two upright pillars supporting the bridge over the road and scattering their loads of stone all over the place, including into the door of an adjoining office.

Little is known for certain about the engines that must have worked so hard pulling 'the empties' from the incline top to Cragg Quarry. Two 0-4-0 saddle tank steam locomotives with the names 'Ant' and 'James'

This odd-looking engine named Ant ended its days at Hutch Bank Quarry but may also well have been the 'Ant' that worked on the Brooks Quarries lines above Cloughfield. *Reproduced by kind permission from The Haslingden Library.*

serving Bagden Quarries (see Walk 18) and was remembered by one lady as pulling up to 12 wagons laden with stone. Two engines called 'Tom' and 'Angel' may also have worked on the line in its early days. An engine with the name 'Alice' or 'Brooks' is also mentioned by the same lady.

Stone traffic was, of course, the raison d'etre of the Brooks Quarries railway but there is a report that supplies for local farms were carried. These supplies were off-loaded at the nearest point to the farm concerned. The children from Foe Edge Farm, just beyond the reversal neck, were regularly given a ride on the railway as far as the embankment under Black Hill from where they walked down to their school at Cowpe in the valley below. There was a passenger service for quarrymen, instigated by a Mrs Brooks (presumably one of the owners or wife thereof), which ran from 'Rope End' (i.e. the top of the incline) to Cragg Quarry. It left early in the morning and returned just after 5.00 p.m. For this service three coaches were built locally.

By 1891, the year of the Ordnance Map 're-survey', the branches from the incline top to Hurdles and Brow Edge Quarries had been lifted but the 'main line' continued in use well into this century. In 1919 there was a quarrymen's strike after which it appears that the railway was not reopened. In 1920 it was reported that the tracks were being torn up.

The Walk

[1] From Bacup Road go south across the River Irwell on Hill End Lane (unfortunately not signposted - it is the southern continuation of Peel Street and Dobbin Lane). Ahead lies the big stone mill building of the Victoria Works of Smith and Nephew. Immediately to the left of the main mill building were the sidings which marked the start of the Brooks Quarries tramway. There was a link over the road on some sort of 'moveable bridge' to a wharf on the north side of the river where stone was transferred to standard gauge wagons on the Hareholme Stone Siding of the Lancashire and Yorkshire Railway. This siding was linked to the main line via a loop line which ran behind Cloughfold Station which was sited immediately west of Hill End Lane on the north side of the river.

Standing just round the bend and looking south between the mill on the right and the row of terraced houses on the left, you can see clearly the course of the tramway climbing steeply uphill. The track on the incline was single with a passing loop in the middle.

The walk now proceeds up the course of the incline. (For those who feel this is too steep, alternative walk A on page 162 is suggested).

[2] Go up the road at the back (the west side) of the row of terraced houses. Near the end go to your right over the grassed area to the wooden stile that gives access to the incline trackbed. Simply follow the incline straight up going over a second wooden stile on the way.

Getting near the halfway point the tramway on the incline went through a cutting. Note that the west side of the cutting is banked with good dressed stone. This is probably a rebuild at sometime after some sort of collapse for the lower east side is revetted with rubble stone only.

[3] At the halfway point a stone wall crosses over the course of the incline. The passing loop was sited immediately the other side of the wall. After being barred at this point for many years the public path on

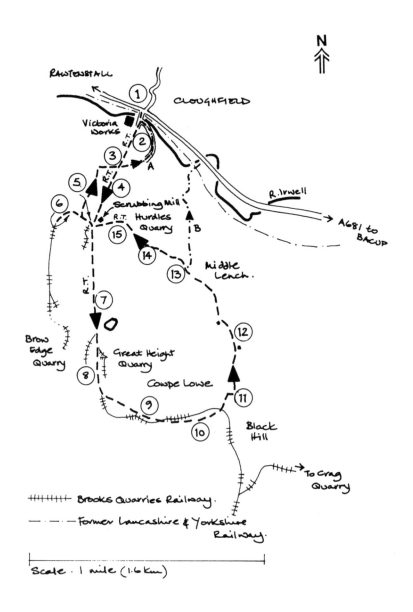

N

RAWTENSTALL
① CLOUGHFIELD
Victoria
Works
R.T. ②
③
A
R.T.
⑤ ④
Scrubbing Mill
⑥ R.T. Hurdles
Quarry B
⑮
⑭
⑬ Middle
Lench.
R.T.
⑦

R. Irwell

A681 to
BACUP

Brow
Edge
Quarry
Great Height
Quarry
⑧
Cowpe Lowe
⑨
⑫
⑪
⑩ Black
Hill

To Crag
Quarry

++++++++ Brooks Quarries Railway.

— – – — Former Lancashire & Yorkshire
Railway.

Scale . 1 mile (1.6 km)

the upper part of the incline has recently been reopened so go over the stile and continue on along the incline trackbed. After about 100 yards the tramway passed over a trackway. The bridge has gone so descend from the embankment you are on to your right.

[4] Once over the trackway climb up onto the embankment on the other side and resume following the incline on its steep climb straight uphill.

[5] At the top you find yourself emerging suddenly onto a wide flat area or platform which is one of the most interesting and evocative spots amongst the many remains connected with the once extensive stone quarrying industry in Rossendale. What a hive of activity this place must once have been. To the left (east) of the incline were the sheds in which flagstones were sawn from massive blocks of stone by framesaws. The rails on which the trolleys carrying the rough blocks of stone to be moved against the framesaws can still be seen. A little further away, remain piles of unwanted off-cuts of stone.

To the west of the incline was the scrubbing or polishing mill. The process of polishing the cut stone was performed by placing the stone on a circular ring of iron. On top of these another set of stones, fastened together by iron bands, were placed. The whole was then made to revolve with each set of stones going in the opposite direction. Evidence of this polishing process can be seen in the large piles of orange yellow sand that run along the crest of the ridge between the incline and the wall to the west. Also to the west of the incline remain piles of slag from the boiler used for raising steam for working the machinery involved in cutting and polishing the stone. Near the edge, west of the incline, are the remains of six cottages.

The incline itself rose to a hump set on an embankment, rising quite high above the middle of the platform, while the assembly sidings were situated at the south end of the platform. The incline itself was self-acting. The ruined building at the south end of the trackbed leading back from the hump probably covered the balance wheel. On the east side of this ruin is a large stone with metal rods sticking out. It looks like some sort of engine housing. Could there have, perhaps, been a stationary engine here to haul the loaded wagons up the steeply graded branch from Hurdles Quarry below to the north east?

It is worthwhile making a diversion along any other branch that led away from the main line to the Brooks tramway system at the incline top, namely, that to Brow Edge Quarry situated about half a mile away to the south south east. This branch left the main line of the system on the east side of the flat area behind the hump of the incline, passing under the incline track immediately to the south of the hump. Be careful not to confuse it with a siding running under the incline in a similar way just to the north of the incline hump. Follow the trackbed of the branch as it then goes westwards crossing the complex remains on the stone works platform. At the west end of the stone yard a stone wall now lies over the trackbed of the branch but a stile enables you to climb over.

High up on the moors, the course of the Brooks Quarries tramway climbs away from the incline head just visible at the end of the cutting. Pendle Hill breaks the horizon beyond.

[6] A few yards on from the stile to the west is a square stone with 'N. 13. 10$^1/_2$ Mill' crudely carved on it. This is believed to be an old locomotive's driver's instruction stone.

The course of the branch tramway then bears round to the left through a cutting at the end of which the line emerged at the top of a high slope giving a fine view over the lower Rossendale Valley. The trackbed of the branch continues terraced out at the top of the slope running southwards for just over a quarter of a mile to reach Brow Edge Quarry. The line to the main part of the quarry ran through a tunnel situated near a much smaller quarry at the north end but, unfortunately, the entrance to this has been covered in. Return now to the incline head to resume the exploration of the main line of the tramway system.

From the area behind the incline hump set off southwards following the course of the main line of the tramway as it passes between two large spoil heaps in a cutting. At the end of the cutting the trackbed of a short branch leading off to a small quarry over to the south west can be seen. Earthworks seem to indicate that the branch had already ceased working before the main line was laid.

The course of the main line is easy to follow as it continues climbing steadily to the south, at first on a low embankment and then through a long cutting.

[7] At the end of the cutting cross over the stile and continue following the course of the tramway. Over on the left are the remains of several quarries, the largest of which was Great Height Quarry situated at the bottom of the slope of Cowpe Lowe. Great Height was working as early as 1866. In 1870 poor John Nuttall, a driver on the tramway to this quarry, lost one of his legs when the seven full wagons being pulled by the horse he was leading got out of control and ran over him as he stumbled in an attempt to get out of the way. Two branches led off to the left to serve this quarry.

[8] A little south of Great Height Quarry and about three-quarters of a mile from the incline top the tramway trackbed passes through a wide gap in the next fence (at the time of writing there was a no gate here). As the right of way leaves the course of the tramway here, you must strike diagonally across the field in a south easterly direction, aiming for the stile next to the white gate on the east side of the field. When you get to the stile, cross over and look back to observe the trackbed of the tramway sweeping round in a wide curve to gain the same position. It must have been an impressive sight indeed in days gone by watching the little steam engines puffing and steaming their way round the curve below to gain the vertical stone side cutting immediately to the south of where you are standing.

[9] Go eastwards along the trackway which is laid with two rows of stone setts for carts carrying stone from the quarry ahead to run on.

Soon, on the right, the tramway trackbed leaves the cutting and crosses the cartway at an acute angle. Leave the stone sett trackway here and go left, following the tramway trackbed.

[10] Ahead you will soon see an impressive embankment which took the tramway in a bend round to the right in front of Black Hill. The course of the tramway can then be seen climbing up the hillside to the south east to a reversal neck from which it launches off to climb to the north east to eventually disappear out of sight behind the top of the slope above Black Hill. An eyewitness remembered five or six tramway wagons once running down the slope behind Black Hill out of control and crashing into the buffers at the end of reversal neck. Cragg Quarry, the main quarry served by the Brooks tramway, lies just over the brow of the hill but this quarry was by no means the furthest point reached by this remarkable tramway. The exploration of that next section, however, is for the next walk.

(Those who wish to walk the whole of the tramway in one go should turn to point 5 of the next walk.)

To start the walk back, go left off the tramway trackbed just before the beginning of the embankment on to the track that bears away to the north east. The track bends a little to the left and brings you to a gate with a stile on the right. Cross over and take the trackway that zigzags downhill to the right.

[11] The track then straightens out to drop down the slope of the hill in a northerly direction and to bring you, after about 300 yards, to a ruined farm. Here leave the trackway and go through the gap at the side of the metal gate on your left. Go to the left of the ruin and then proceed straight on, keeping the wire fence on your left.

[12] After about 100 yards a stone wall crosses the line of the path. The path passes through this wall by a gap which is about 20 paces down from the wire fence and is not visible until you are almost level with it.

Continue on with the barbed wire fence on you left until another stile, just to the right of another ruin, appears ahead. Cross over this stile, go past the north side of the ruin and then strike northwards diagonally across the field, making for a gap in a jutting out section of the tumbled stone wall below you. Go through the gap and follow the wall on your right for a few yards downhill until a faint green trackway comes through the same wall. Turn left and follow this trackway as it goes to the north west, dropping gently towards Middle Lench Farm.

[13] When you get to the farm turn right through the gate and make your way through the farmyard to the farm road. (Here those who want the shortest way back and no more climbing should take Alternative Route B on page 162)

Turn left on the farm road and proceed westwards until you come to the last house of the hamlet. Go left here, round the south side of the house and then continue on along the trackway that goes up the hill to the west. Ignore the trackway that goes off to the left after a few paces. Instead keep straight on to the north west on the stone slabbed way that soon brings you to Hurdles Quarry.

[14] Hurdles Quarry, like many of the larger stone quarries in Rossendale, cuts into the hillside, following the beds of Haslingden Flags, a sandstone formed in ancient river deltas about 320 million years ago. Here the open face method was used. In other words, the rock face was cut into, with the required stone being removed, while the unwanted rock or overburden was dumped behind on the platform made by earlier stone removal. Some stone was, no doubt, taken out of the quarry by road and also, according to one source, by aerial ropeway. Much stone, however, must have gone out via the tramway which ran from the west end of the quarry uphill to the scrubbing mill and stone yard above Cloughfold. The tramway was lifted and the quarry apparently disused by 1891.

[15] Go through the quarry on the trackway that runs between the quarry face and the mounds of overburden. The tramway trackbed becomes clear when you get to the west end of the quarry. Follow the trackbed here as it bends to the left on open hillside, climbing uphill, first on an embankment and then through a cutting, to reach the stone yard covered earlier on the walk. It remains an open question as to whether this branch was worked as a powered incline or by adhesive traction. If it was by the latter method, only one or two loaded wagons could have been brought up at a time.

Make your way across the former stone yard to the west, following the trackbed of the Brow Edge Quarry branch until you come to the stone wall and stile. This time do not cross over but turn right and proceed northwards, keeping the stone wall on your left. The track goes downhill and then bends to the right to take you past Hill End which you passed near on the outward walk. From here simply follow the farm road back to the bottom of the valley and the start of the walk.

Alternative A

Proceed along Hill End Lane as it leads away to the south east soon bending to the right to climb uphill past a group of terraced houses known as Upper Ashmount. After about a quarter of a mile, where a farm road goes off to the left, a gate and stile lie across the lane. Cross over the stile and go along the track that leads to the west to Hill End ahead.

The bed of the incline can be clearly seen coming up steeply on your right to cross over the trackway on the level. The passing loop was just over the wall on your left.

Pass on to the left of Hill End, go over the stile by the west end of the house and continue on the trackway up hill. Continue following the trackway where it bends left to run south, ignoring the stile in the wall at the bend. About 400 yards further on you come to a big flat area with the hump of the incline rising in the middle. Make your way across and resume reading the description of the main walk at point 5 on page 157.

Alternative B

Turn right on the farm road and follow it downhill for just over a quarter of a mile. Just in front of some mills near the bottom you come to the trackbed of the former Ramsbottom to Bacup Railway which is now part of the Irwell Way. Go left over the new wooden stile and go along the Irwell Way which after just under a half mile will bring you back to the start of the walk.

Walk 16: The Brooks Quarries Lines - Black Hill to Ding

Map:Pathfinder Maps 690 SD 82/92 and 701 SD 81/91

Distance: $5^1/_2$ miles.

Start: In Cowpe Village in Rossendale at the big Cowpe Sunday School building. Grid reference SD 838 209.

By Car: From.Rawtenstall (for directions see Walk 15) go east on the A681 road to Bacup. $1^1/_2$ miles from Rawtenstall, immediately after the traffic lights in the centre of Waterfoot, take the first turning right for the road to Cowpe. The Sunday School building, which looks like a Free Church chapel, is on the west side of the road about $1/_2$ mile from Waterfoot. Just over 200 yards south of the Sunday School building and next to the recreation field the road is wide enough for parking.

By Public Transport: Frequent bus service to Waterfoot from Rawtenstall and Bacup as well as a less frequent service from Rawtenstall to Cowpe.

This is the second of two walks following the remains of the Brooks Quarries tramway system. While involving one major climb, this walk is rewarding on a clear day for its views as well as for its railway interest. The walk is over field paths, trackways and a little rough moor.

The Railway

The general story of the Brooks and Brooks quarries tramway system has been outlined in the introduction to Walk 15. This walk will follow the tramway from the reversal neck near Black Hill to its furthest point reached, namely, Ding Quarry over on the Rochdale side of Hailstorm Hill. In between these two points lay Cragg Quarry which was the largest quarry served by the tramway. From Cragg Quarry the tramway reached over the watershed to Ding Quarry via two inclines which met at the top and where they shared the same stationary steam haulage engine. By the very nature of things the two inclines could not be self-acting for, not only was there the expected traffic of stone to be hauled up from Ding Quarry on its way to the scrubbing mill above Cloughfold, but there was also some traffic of stone from the Cragg Quarry side to go over to Ding where, presumably, it was loaded into road carts to be taken to Rochdale. For some reason the course of the incline on the Ding side was altered sometime between 1891 and 1909.

It is possible that the inclines between Cragg and Ding Quarries were closed before the rest of the tramway system in about 1919 as the bottom part of the northern incline, which was situated in Cragg Quarry, has been cut away by later quarrying. This may, however, have happened during limited quarrying after 1919 and, anyway, we do know it was still there in 1909. Ding Quarry itself continued to be worked long after the tramway closed and this has destroyed the bottom parts of even the later southern incline. Apart from this the incline as well as the trackbed of the tramway system in Cragg Quarry, are well preserved.

The Walk

[1] Take the farm road that leads off to the south west to the left of the Sunday School building (there is a bungalow on the other side of the farm road). Follow the farm road until, after passing a stone house on the left, it bends to the right to end in front of a second stone house.

[2] Go on, keeping this second house with its barn on your left, making for the gap stile to the right of the gate ahead. After passing through take the path which keeps straight on. This keeps slightly uphill in a north westerly direction immediately to the left of the wall running in the same direction.

[3] After about 200 yards you will come to a metal gate in the wall on your right with a tractor track passing through it to make its way, after a sharp left-hand bend, uphill in a southerly direction. Turn left and follow this track until you come to a gate across the track (don't be misled into taking a minor branch which goes into the field on the right). Pass through the gate and follow the track as it bends to the right for about a further 150 yards.

[4] Be careful here. Do not follow the more used track which turns sharp left to climb steeply uphill. Instead take the right-hand, lesser used track

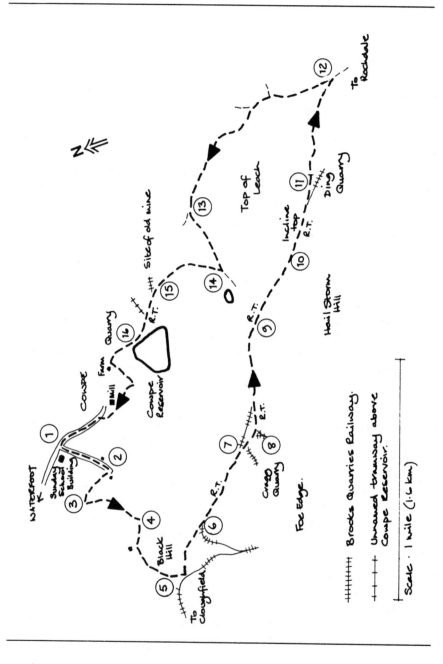

which, after following a tumbled wall on the right, turns to the left (by a ruin on the right) to climb up the hill in a westerly direction.

[5] At the top of the hill this track ends at a gate with a stile to the left. Cross over the stile. The embankment of the Brooks quarries tramway, as it curves beneath Black Hill, looms ahead. This is the same embankment which was viewed from a different angle on the previous walk. Go straight on for just over 100 yards till, just by the south east end of the tramway embankment, you come to another trackway which crosses the one you are on at an oblique angle. Turn left onto this trackway and follow it as it winds its way uphill round the south side of Black Hill. On your right, as you proceed, you will have a good view of the course of the tramway as it runs along a stone revetted embankment climbing uphill to the reversal neck just out of sight round the bend on the hillside. The line of the tramway can be observed reappearing at a slightly higher level on the same hillside running at first on a terrace and then on a low embankment to eventually join the same track that you are on further up the hill. Continue on the trackway to this joining point.

[6] The point where the tramway joined the trackway is opposite a metal gate on the left in the stone wall to the north. The stone slabs end where the tramway comes in. It appears that from here onward the carts and the tramway used the same way or, more probably, road cartage ceased when the railway was opened and the stone slabs were taken up for the wooden sleepers of the tramway to be laid in their place.

Continue along the trackbed as it pushes on south eastwards preparing to dive into the numerous mounds formed by the overburden or waste from the quarry workings. Several branches ran off from the main line to the right. The first of these branches runs off in front of the first mound. As you proceed on, in the numerous cuttings through the mounds, try to visualise the numerous trestles which carried temporary tramways from the open quarry face and mine holes (Cragg Quarry was not just opencast working) over the main line to the edge of the tip overhanging Cowpe Valley below.

[7] After about 200 yards the mounds on the left end and one has a marvellous view to the north over Cowpe and middle Rossendale, while on a clear day Pen-y-Ghent in the Yorkshire Dales can be seen. About here the trackbed of the main line branches slightly away to the right from the present trackway. Follow the course of the main line as it

bends round a little to the right. Note the remains of a branch tramway coming in on the right at a slightly higher level to form a trailing junction further on.

[8] The main line then bends round to the left, emerging into a wide flat area where the remains of loading platforms and the course of another branch to the right can be observed. The latter appears to have joined the main line in a triangular shaped junction. It has been suggested that this was used for turning locomotives but this seems unlikely as detailed maps showing the track layout above Cloughfold show no triangle there.

The Brooks Quarries tramway makes a wide sweep on the high embankment on the right while the old cart road takes a shorter route on the left. View from between points 5 and 6 of the walk.

From this flat area follow the trackbed of the main line of the tramway as it resumes a straight course in a south easterly direction soon to join the present trackway again. Follow the trackway until just after a slight bend to the right it bends to the left and begins to drop down.

[9] The main line here continued straight on to climb up the side of

Cowpe Moss via an incline. Unfortunately, the bottom section of the incline has been damaged by later quarrying and the embankment you are on now comes to a sudden end. A mound on the right enables you get up onto the edge ahead formed by later quarrying. Next go left along the edge until you come to a point formed by an imaginary extension of the embankment you have just been on to the edge you are on. Here you are on the course of the incline. Follow the course of the incline as it goes uphill in a south easterly direction. The surface of the incline, although not too obvious at this point, can be picked out because it is covered with grass in contrast to the surrounding moor which is covered in heather.

After crossing a little embankment the trackbed of the incline bends a little to the right. From here one can pick out the incline more easily as it climbs to the top of the moor. Continue on up the trackbed as it goes over two short embankments formed of massive chunks of roughly quarried rock tipped down in an apparently random way.

[10] At the top of the incline the two humps to stop wagons rolling back downhill and the foundations of the engine house are still clearly visible. Over on the right a mound formed of clinker from the boiler of the stationary engine can be seen. What a bleak place this was for the engine man in the depths of winter.

On the southern side of the moor the incline leading down to Ding Quarry can be easily made out. Follow this downhill.

About halfway down you will come to a low stone platform on the left. This appears to have been placed here in order to enable coal to be loaded onto railway wagons from a drift mine a little further over to the left. At this point the incline appears to divide. The left-hand or more northerly of the two routes is the newer one, replacing the right-hand or more southerly original route somewhere between 1891 and 1909. Continue on down, using the left-hand incline course.

[11] You will soon find yourself at the edge of Ding Quarry. From here you have a good view over the quarry but, unfortunately, as you can see, later quarrying has completely obliterated any trace of the bottom of either incline route. So the end is reached of this remarkable but sadly little documented and little known English narrow gauge railway. Indeed, it was a remarkable Victorian piece of engineering.

Proceed carefully along the edge of the quarry until a slope enables you to make your way down into the quarry and join a well defined trackway which goes off in an easterly and then a south easterly direction.

[12] After about a third of a mile you come to Rooley Moor Road, which is surfaced with hard stone setts. Here turn left and follow this road as it makes its way first northwards and then north westwards across the moor.

[13] After just under a mile, as the Cowpe Valley comes into view again, you come to a fork in the road. Take the left-hand track; that is the one with the line of two parallel large stone setts. Ahead lies the tip of overburden from the east end of Cragg Quarry.

[14] Continue on the stone sett way for about 400 yards until, just after going through a gap in a quarry tip, you come to a track coming in sharply on your right. Turn right onto this track and follow it as it goes gently downhill in a north easterly and then northerly direction.

[15] After about an eighth of a mile, just past a small iron railed enclosure on your right, you will notice on your left a large cement slab. About 35 paces beyond this you come to the remains of an incline which ran from a drift mine over to your right down to the bottom of the valley. Go left off the trackway and follow this incline downhill.

Just before you reach the stone wall ahead you may notice what appears to be the trackbed of a branch line going off to your right. This line, which ran to a quarry about 250 yards to the right, was probably worked by horses. From the junction with this branch the incline starts to drop more steeply downhill. Go through the wicket gate in the wall ahead and continue on downhill on the incline until you come to a wire fence.

From here onwards the course of the incline has been obscured by the earthworks of Cowpe Reservoir which was constructed between 1898 and 1904. Proceed along to the north with the fence on your left until it bends away to the north west and downhill. Here go straight on.

[16] Soon you will find yourself in an old quarry. Pick up the trackway which leads north westwards out of the quarry to a farm. At the gate to the farmyard go left and take the path that leads downhill by the side of the reservoir to the left of a stone wall. At the bottom turn right on to

the tarmac road which links the reservoir works to the village of Cowpe. When you come to the T-junction turn left and you will soon find yourself back at the start of the walk.

Walk 17: The Quarry Lines of East Rossendale

Map:Pathfinder Maps 690 SD 82/92 and 701 SD 81/91

Distance: about 5 miles.

Start: The main car park at Stacksteads in the Rossendale Valley between Rawtenstall and Bacup. Grid reference SD 853 217.

By Car: Coming.from the south the best approach is via the M66 and its A56 and A682 dual carriageway extensiion aiming for Rawtenstall. Leave Rawtenstall on the A681 road to Bacup. Stacksteads is on this road 2 $^1/_2$ miles east of Rawtenstall. The car park is in the middle of Stacksteads on the north side of the road just past the parish church (spire).

By Public Transport: There is a regular service of buses from Rawtenstall and Bacup.

This walk explores the remains of no less than three railway systems which served the numerous quarries in the hills of the eastern part of Rossendale. Even if at the end of the walk you are left somewhat confused and a little perplexed as to how all the systems fitted in with each other with regard to time, place and method of working, you will at least have gained an impression of the immense spread of rail served workings that covered this area during the late Victorian era. Despite considerable damage to the lower end of one of the systems by recent 'land reclamation', the railways have left much evidence of their once very active existence.

Much of the walk is over open moor, so chose a clear day and suitable footwear.

The Railways

The first railway system met with is that which served the several quarries owned by Richard Siddall. This standard gauge line led from

This view of 'Tam o'Shanter' at Facit Quarry near Whitworth could be at any of the quarries served by the standard gauge quarry railways on the hills of the east of Rossendale. *Reproduced by kind permission from The Rawtenstall Library.*

'Siddall's Sidings' on the Ramsbottom to Bacup line of the Lancashire and Yorkshire Railway just east of Stacksteads Station. The line climbed for one-and-a-half miles over the hills to the south via three inclines to Back Cowm Quarry which was the furthest out of the several quarries served by the system.

The first of the inclines is described as having a 'steam drum' which was necessary because the lighter gradient on part of the incline did not allow the loaded descending wagons to completely pull the empty ascending wagons right to the top. Usually two wagons went up as two came down. There were several accidents on the incline. One such was in 1884 when the wire rope broke and the loaded wagons hurtled down, crashing into a stone wall at the bottom and hurling their load of stones on to the Lancashire and Yorkshire Railway line just as the 7.50 a.m. train from Bacup was coming into sight. Fortunately, the passenger train was able to stop before meeting the unexpected obstruction. The scrubbing mill, unlike on the Brooks Quarry Railway at Cloughfold, was near the sidings at the bottom of the incline.

'Lymm', here posing at Facit Quarry, also worked at Brandwood Quarry above Stacksteads. *Reproduced by kind permission from The Rawtenstall Library.*

A standard gauge engine waits for trucks to arrive up the wire rope incline. Probable location near point 8 of the walk. *Reproduced by kind permission from The Bacup Library.*

There were four 0-6-0 saddle tank (one might have been a side tank) steam locomotives on this system. There was also one 0-4-0 tank engine called 'Frost Holes' which is believed to have been a vertical- boilered 'coffee pot'.

Firm dates are hard to come by but the accident described above tells us, of course, that the lower part of the railway system was operating at least by 1884. A newspaper report in 1883 states that Richard Siddall was busy, laying a 'new tramway'. There is a reference to a workman being killed at Back Cowm Quarry in 1888. The Ordnance Survey map of 1891 shows the railway laid as far as the top of the third incline, though not as far as Back Cowm Quarry itself. The same map, however, shows what seems likely to be an empty trackbed running to the quarry so it seems that by this date Back Cowm had switched its stone traffic to the Britannia Quarry outlet (see below) to which it is already shown connected by rail on the same map. It appears, therefore, that the Back Cowm section had a very short life.

The Ordnance Survey map of 1909 shows that the railway had been

This scene at a standard gauge served Rossendale stone quarry illustrates well the activity at the quarry face. Note the steam crane on broad gauge tracks. *Reproduced by kind permission from the Bacup Library.*

shortened a little and that it was now linked at its southern end to a shaft through which, no doubt, stone was raised from the network of underground stone mines under the moor. A sale advertised in 1914 as 'account of Richard Siddall - deceased' mentioned no less than seven miles of railway. In 1944 Frost Holes Quarry, the quarry nearest to the main line sidings, was offered for sale. It seems that the railway had closed quite a few years before.

The second of the railway system remains to be explored by this walk are those of a standard gauge system stemming from an incline linking the system to the former Lancashire and Yorkshire Railway's Rochdale to Bacup line at Britannia. The system serviced a group of quarries collectively known as Britannia Quarries, although they were just over the watershed on the Whitworth side of the hills south of Bacup.

The incline, which began immediately west of Britannia Station, was of the self-acting type and controlled by a ten foot diameter drum. There were three rails on the incline so that the wagons ascending and descending shared the middle rail except at the middle where there was a passing loop. Dates again are not easy to come by but the incline was certainly in use by 1887 when the rope broke and some loaded wagons came free smashing into a wall at the bottom.

The incline serviced two major quarries. The first of these and the furthest away at about one-and-a-half miles, was Hall Cowm Quarry which was owned by Butterworth and Brooks, later Brooks and Brooks, who also owned the three foot gauge railway system above Cloughfold (see Walk 15). Back Cowm Quarry, which was once serviced by Richard Siddall's railway mentioned above, seems to have been absorbed quite early on into this quarry. The other quarry serviced by the Britannia incline was Height End Quarry which was owned by the Heys family who also owned several other quarries. in the district.

Both quarries had their own steam locomotives which were shedded separately. The Heys quarry was known to have had three engines, two of which were 0-4-0 saddle tanks and the other one an 0-6-0 saddle tank. The Brooks quarry had four locomotives, namely, three 0-6-0 and one 0-4-0, of which three at least were saddle tanks.

At some date between 1881 and 1909 Lee Quarry, Stacksteads, was linked to the Britannia Quarries railway system by a three-quarters of a mile branch which ran westwards to the quarry from the incline top.

The Britannia Quarries system lasted much longer than most of the other Rossendale quarry railway systems. B. Roberts in 'Railways and Mineral Tramways of Rossendale' states that locomotive operation creased about 1943 but shows a locomotive in steam in a snow filled cutting on a photograph dated 'c.1946'. In the autumn of 1946 a lecturer on local history talking about the incline describes it as 'now dismantled'. Part of the Britannia Quarries still has stone being quarried, but, alas, all the products now go out by road.

The third quarry railway system whose remains will be seen on the walk is that which served Lee Quarries south of Bacup. The quarries, which were operated by more than one firm, had their main outlet via a self-acting incline of just under half a mile length which ran from the lip of one of the quarries down to a wharf alongside the Lancashire and Yorkshire Railway's Ramsbottom to Bacup line, just west of the southern entrance to the tunnel south of Bacup Station. The railway on the incline was, according to B. Roberts, of the unusual gauge of three foot three inches, though a newspaper, describing an accident with a runaway wagon being moved by a horse in one of the quarries, states the gauge to be three foot six inches.

In 1878 the letting was offered for the building of the retaining wall and piers for 'Lee Tramway', while in 1880 the 'new tramway' was described as ready for opening. The incline had its usual crop of accidents. One such was in 1907 when an empty wagon came free on the incline and crashed into the river at the bottom after being switched off the main line. In 1936 the 'haulage drum' at the top of the incline, with the building which housed it, were destroyed by fire, The newspaper report of this fire described the firemen as being handicapped by the remote situation of the building. The incline closed about 1942.

It appears that one of the Lee Quarries had an internal two foot gauge railway system worked by a petrol locomotive.

As we have seen, Lee Quarries was also later served by a standard gauge outlet via the Britannia incline, while in the earlier period the western end of the quarries was serviced by a branch from Richard Siddall's line to Stacksteads. The latter had gone by 1909.

On the walk you will come across yet another incline. This ran from Greens Moor Quarry to a road serviced wharf at Holm Bank near the entrance to Bacup cemetery. There was also a link from Greens Moor Quarry to Richard Siddall's line to his sidings at Stacksteads Station. As this link is shown on the Ordnance Survey map of 1891 as connected with the line running to the incline, we can assume that the railway on the incline was of standard gauge. The rails on the incline had been lifted by 1909.

The Walk

[1] From the west end of the car park make your way across Newchurch Road and go south through the wide gap between the hairdressers and Boys' Funeral Parlour.

Almost immediately past the houses you cross the course of the former railway between Rawtenstall and Bacup (Stacksteads Station was sited about 150 yards to the west). Bearing slightly left and aiming for the footbridge over the Irwell to the south, you next cross the site of 'Siddall's Sidings' where Richard Sidall's standard gauge quarry tramway began. Unfortunately, because of land 'improvements', nothing is left here to remind us of either the railway or the tramway.

[2] Make your way over the river by the footbridge. Here the tramway crossed over the river and then made its way to the south going straight uphill on an incline (power-assisted - see introduction), while to the right, immediately south of the bridge, a branch led off to Frost Holes Quarry which is now completely filled in and obscured.

On the south side of the footbridge don't go right on the main path but cross over the stile and go straight uphill, between the wooden fences. This path is on the course of the former incline of Siddall's tramway but, alas, land 'reclamation' has again obliterated any traces but don't despair the 'reclamation' work will soon end.

[3] After about 250 yards the path levels out and you come to a stile which gives access to an unmetalled road. Cross over and look over the stone wall opposite. At long last unreclaimed land is reached and the course of Richard Siddall's tramway can now be seen in a hollow running eastwards.

Turn right and follow the road westwards for about 100 yards until you come to two attached stone houses. Go left round these until you come

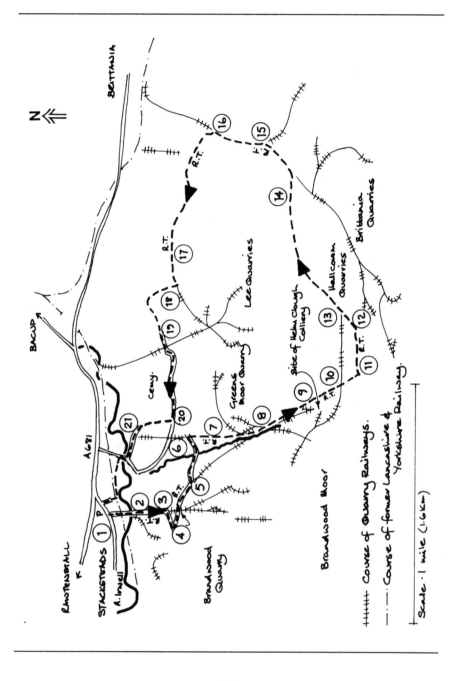

right round on the other side and then take the trackway that goes off to the south east and not the one that goes off to the south.

[4] About 100 yards along this trackway you will find yourself standing over the course of Siddall's tramway. Its trackbed can be seen running from underneath the trackway you are on in a southerly direction towards a large quarry to the south. Only the eastern end of this quarry was served by Siddall's tramway; the central and western sections, known as Brandwood Quarry, were served by a separate standard gauge tramway belonging to Henry Heys. This tramway had its exchange sidings with the Lancashire and Yorkshire Railway about a third of a mile west of the Siddall tramway sidings.

High up above Stacksteads in Rossendale are the substantial remains of Richard Siddall's quarry railway. Here it clings precariously to the hillside at about the half-way point of the second incline.

Just to the north of where you are standing was the top of the first incline of Siddall's tramway. From this incline top the line bore away on a curve to the east to link up with the second incline which led off to the south east taking the tramway further up the hill side. Just from the south to the west of where you are standing the Ordnance Survey map of 1891 shows several sidings with some cranes. Here then, most likely,

179

stone from the quarries up on the hillside would have been cut and dressed. A glance at the map will show that wagons could gave got from one incline to the other by going via a double reversal through these sidings as well as directly via the above mentioned curve.

Continue now on the trackway as it climbs gently at first to the south east. The trackway is laid on the trackbed of the tramway as is evidenced by the low embankment you soon find yourself walking on. As you proceed, a glance to your right will reveal on the hillside, the remains of another incline climbing steeply to a small quarry sited high above the east end of the main Brandwood Quarry.

[5] When you reach the hamlet of Greens on your left you must leave the incline trackbed to take the track that goes off to the middle of the hamlet. Note the remains of the bridge that once carried the tramway over an old trackway going straight up the hillside (but don't go up this trackway). Immediately beyond was the halfway passing loop of the incline which continued on up the hillside a little to the left of the old trackway. It is not very clear from this angle but you will get a much better view of the upper section further on.

Go between the two houses on your left into the middle of the hamlet. Here, ignoring the road that goes off to the left, continue straight on into the farmyard in front of you; a wooden footpath sign points the way. Turn right immediately past the farmhouse. After a few paces, having gone through a gate, turn left into narrow green lane. Follow this green lane as it leads eastwards (via a gate with a stile next to it) to drop down to cross the stream in Greens Clough. Over on your right the waste tips of Greens Moor Quarry rise menacingly above reminiscent of the waste tips of Welsh slate quarries. Cross the stream and go up the other side, keeping to the left of the wire fence that comes down to the stream.

[6] After the wire fence ends you find yourself between two stone walls. Here you are under what used to be the bridge of a long incline which carried stone from Richard Siddall's Greens Moor Quarry downhill to a road-served staith at Holm Bank, Stacksteads. The end of this walk will take you past the lower end of this incline. This incline is shown on the Ordnance Survey map of 1891 but had had its track lifted by the time of the 1909 survey. Climb up onto the trackbed of the incline and make your way southwards and uphill, following the course of the incline.

After a bit of puff you cross a stile. Then after a few yards the trackbed of the incline is obscured by later quarry tipping. The path, however, is clear and easy to follow as it continues upwards over these tippings.

[7] As you proceed, on your right you have a good view of the course of the main line of Siddall's tramway as it climbs up from Law Head and Greens on an inclined plane to the head of the incline on Greens Moor. The half-way point of the incline, where the ascending and descending wagons would pass, was situated just opposite you where the trackbed widens out and levels off a little. The course of the tramway can then be seen running, terraced out, on the steep west slope of Greens Clough or Hell Clough as it is often locally known. Note the stone revetting of the side of the tramway terrace recalling work on similar tramways of about the same period in North Wales.

The path now levels off. The head of the incline down to Holm Bank was about somewhere here but of this there is no sign now.

Continue along the path as it runs south eastwards just above the stream. On the other side the course of the main line of Siddall's tramway reaches the same level as your path and turns slightly to cross the stream to the side you are on. Here a reversal enabled the tramway to reach the works area of Richard Siddall's Greens Moor Quarry which stretched away to the east. Unfortunately, later workings have completely obliterated all the evidence in this area.

[8] A few yards beyond, where the tramway crossed over the stream, you will notice on the west side of the Clough the remains of an incline leading up the slope in a southerly direction. Once over the lip of the Clough this branch tramway proceed up the more gentle slope of Greens Moor to a drift mine where, no doubt, coal would have been brought out just before the turn of the century.

Continue on the upper path that goes in a south easterly direction on the east side of the stream. Below you the course of the branch tramway to Helm Clough Colliery can easily be made out as it hugs the east side of the stream. On the other side you will notice the remains of a second short incline rising up from the bottom of the clough but going this time in a north easterly direction. This one is a bit of a mystery as the track bed extends only for about 30 yards beyond the lip of the clough and ends in the middle of rough moor without any sign of a drift mine or shaft. Was there some change of plan after the earthworks had been started? Opposite the point where this second short incline would have crossed the stream (the abutments of the bridge remain) there remains the entrance to a small level or drift mine.

[9] As you proceed, the course of the upper or main line of the tramway once more becomes clear. Soon a second link, leading sharply downhill on the right, to Helm Clough Colliery can be seen. The site of the colliery itself with the entrance to its 'level' can be easily made out. The colliery appears to have been served by an earlier tramway, the course of which can be seen crossing the stream and bearing away in a north westerly direction on an embankment. Just beyond here it joins (via a reversal) what appears to be the course of another tramway which served another colliery away to the west. This tramway, which we will call for convenience the Brandwood Moor tramway, then bore away to the south east recrossing the stream further to the south on another embankment and then making its way across the moor to the south east.

Continue along the course of Siddall's tramway as it climbs steadily uphill in a straight line, passing through a long but shallow cutting.

[10] On your left, at the end of the cutting, is a ring of large chunks of stone and rock looking like some freshly built Iron Age fort which has suddenly appeared on the moor. The ring, in fact, marks the top of a former mine out of the shaft of which good quality stone cut out in underground galleries was brought to the surface. Indeed, this shaft was probably one of the outlets for the once extensive underground workings that spread out under this moor. The top of the brick line shaft of this mine is still visible in the middle of the ring. The shaft was sunk sometime after 1891 and was in use in 1909. On the south side of the ring of stone the trackbed of a short branch linking this mine to the main line of Siddall's tramway can be seen.

Just to the south of the mine the Brandwood Moor tramway crossed over the course of Siddall's tramway. An examination of the actual crossing point will reveal that the trackbed of the Brandwood Moor tramway is a little higher than that of Siddall's tramway. This seem to indicate that the Brandwood Moor line was older than Siddall's line and that it had already closed before the latter was made.

Continue following the course of Siddall's tramway as it climbs steadily, following a straight line to the south east.

[11] At the highest point you come to the stone foundation of what was possibly the stationary engine for hauling wagons up from Hall Cowm Quarries over to the east. Leading away downhill to the south east is the trackbed of some sort of well laid way. Was this once a tramway? It seems far too narrow to have been a standard gauge tramway, as was Siddall's tramway, yet the straightness and the cutting it passes through, before dropping down into Robin Hood's Well Clough beyond, have a tramway feel about them. Could it have been a narrow gauge tramway but if so why the change of gauge?

A short diversionary walk down this trackbed (of whatever origin) will enable you to look down into Robin Hoods Well Clough with the remains of stone workings to the east and a drift coal mine opposite. This colliery was served in 1909 by tramway whose course can be seen running away to the west to link up with the Hall Cowm Quarries system.

Back at the site of the stationary engine at the incline top, if you look to the north, you can see, bending away to the east, the trackbed of a tramway aiming for Hall Cowm Quarries. This tramway, the course of which is clearly of standard gauge width, was most likely the route by which Richard Siddall brought stone up from his Back Cowm Quarries to pass down via the tramway you have just followed into Stacksteads.

The walk now continues following the course of this tramway. About 250 yards from the start, notice the short branch leading off to the left to what was probably a coal mine entered by a level.

[12] A little further on the trackbed widens for a short section. Here, in all likelihood, was the halfway point of the incline. Then, a few yards further on, the trackbed suddenly ends and you find yourself overlooking the later quarry workings which have destroyed the evidence of the bottom end of this incline. As you contemplate the maze of workings of Hall Cowm and Britannia Quarries, a look to the south east will enable you to pick out the course of the later tramway running from the colliery in Robin Hood's Well Clough as it threads its way through cuttings in the vast quarry tips, making for the two high stone towers in the distance which mark the centre of the former Hall Cowm Quarries.

Turn left and make your way for about a mile to the north east skirting along the northerly edge of the quarry working, taking special care near the steeper edges.

[13] After about 100 yards you cross a hollow way which also disappears as it runs eastwards into the later quarry workings,. This was the course of Brandwood Moor tramway (if such it was). Here it is about a quarter of a mile east of the crossing with Siddall's tramway which you saw earlier. Continue along the northerly edge of the workings in a north easterly direction.

[14] Eventually, at a point immediately to the north of the 'tower' of modern quarry machinery and by three old telegraph-poles, you will come to a small square enclosure round an old pit shaft. From here you can pick up a good surfaced trackway leading off to the east. This trackway may well mark the course of a tramway once serving the pit.

Soon the trackway turns a little to the left and joins the course of another trackway. Here you are now on the course of the main line of the standard gauge Britannia Quarries tramway which also later served Hall Cowm Quarries. A glance to the right will reveal a shallow cutting before the tramway trackbed disappears into the modern quarry workings. Continue north eastwards, following the tramway trackbed. Note the remains of a loading bay which soon appears on the left.

[15] The trackbed soon bends to the left to enter a cutting which, however, is unfortunately, after a few yards, partly filled with rubble. This will, no doubt, confuse industrial archaeologists of some future generation.

A little further on, about 40 paces south of the boundary marker and the start of a stone wall on your left, careful looking on your right will reveal the trackbed of a branch coming in from the south east. The junction with main line has been disturbed but just a little back some wooden sleepers are still in place, but rapidly rotting away. The branch tramway served a number of shafts out of which good quality stone from underground galleries was brought up. The furthest of these was a quarter of a mile away.

[16] Once over the brow of the hill a stile over a fence and to the right of a gate across the trackway appears. Cross over the stile and you, will find yourself standing on the top of the Britannia Quarries tramway incline. Enough remains to give some idea of how the top of this self-acting incline was laid out. From the hump you have a good view down the hill to the incline bottom where the tramway made a right-hand bend to reach the sidings which linked it to the former

Lancashire and Yorkshire Railway's Rochdale to Bacup line.

The suggested way back goes along the trackbed of the branch tramway which ran from the top of the incline along the contour in a westerly direction to Lee Quarries. Facing northwards, the branch moved off to the left. Unfortunately, the start has been obscured by some recent works. Once back over the stile, you must work your way round the south side of the new wooden fenced enclosure until, on the west side you meet a wire fence. From here you can follow the trackbed of the Lee Quarries branch without any difficulty.

As you proceed westwards, there are some good views of the upper part of the Rossendale Valley. Do also look down and you will notice several wooden sleepers still in their original places.

[17] After just over half a mile and opposite the first of the quarry mounds on your left, a stone wall comes up from your right to run alongside the trackbed. Where this wall makes a junction with two other walls (just by a stile in the wall on your left) be careful not to be diverted by a trackway going off slightly to the left following the stone wall which goes off to the south west. Keep straight on here. The odd, almost buried, sleeper will prove that you are still on the tramway trackbed.

[18] After about 150 yards the fence on your right turns through 90 degrees to make its way downhill. Here the course of the tramway you are on crosses what appears to be the remains of a tramway going a downhill. The main tramway can be seen going on to the left through a cutting in a waste tip mound. Beyond this later quarry workings have destroyed any trace (there is a right of way up to the cutting if you wish to explore further).

Go down the slope, keeping the wire fence on your right. At the bottom of the slope go left onto the farm track.

[19] After about 350 yards, and just after passing Lee Farmhouse on your right, the track you are on crosses the remains of yet another incline. This incline (three foot three inch gauge and self-acting) provided the first and main link from the Lee Quarries to the Lancashire and Yorkshire Railway in the valley below. The course of the railway can be clearly made out going downhill to the bottom where it bent to the right to some stone cutting works and to what was known as Holt's Sidings.

Once across the course of the incline continue straight on in a westerly direction, crossing the left one of the two stiles facing you and going down the rush filled green lane. Follow the lane as it bends left to cross Lee Clough and then climbs up the other side. After passing Fairwell Farm on the right it becomes a hard surfaced lane.

[20] Follow the lane until on your right, you come to some garages situated just beyond the row of terraced houses on your left. Go through the gap between these garages to pick up the path that goes down the slope in a northerly direction.

As you go down this path, note that the houses on your left are situated above the remains a stone embankment. This embankment formed part of the Greens Moor Quarry to Holm Bank incline which you came across on the earlier part of the walk.

[21] The path ends opposite the gateway to a cemetery. Turn left into the road here. Almost straightaway on your left you will see a monumental stonemason's yard. This yard is situated on the site of the staith of the incline from Greens Moor Quarry. Here stone from the quarry would have been loaded into carts for local road distribution.

When you come to a T-junction turn right to cross the River Irwell. Immediately over the bridge turn left and go along the unmetalled road that runs to the west along the north bank of the river.

The road brings you to a sports field. Turn right and make you way round the north side of the field and to the south of the embankment of the former Rawtenstall to Bacup Railway. At the end of the field turn right and follow the lane to the north which will bring you back to the start of the walk at Stacksteads car park.

Walk 18: The Bagden Quarry Railway

Map: Pathfinder Map 701 SD 81/91

Distance: $4^1/_2$ miles.

Start: The main entrance to Healey Dell Nature Reserve on the A671 Rochdale to Bacup road about 2 miles north of Rochdale. Grid reference SD 883 159.

By Car: The entrance to Healey Dell Nature Reserve, with a large sign, is on the west side of the road on a sharp bend just past the Rossendale boundary sign (if coming from Rochdale). There is room for cars to park on the north side of Shawclough Road (B6377) which leads away to the west from the entrance to Healey Dell.

By Public Transport: There is a frequent bus service to Healey Dell from both Rochdale and Bacup.

This is stimulating walk on a fresh day, taking the hill railway explorer high up on the moor. Just one not too long steep climb but the ground underfoot can be very wet in parts, even in summer.

The Railway

The Bagden Quarry line was a three foot gauge tramway with a length of one-and-three-quarters miles, of which approximately half was on an incline. The tramway started a little north of Broadley Station on the Lancashire and Yorkshire Railway's Rochdale to Bacup line. From the wharf on the latter railway it climbed via a self-acting incline (three rails with passing loop type) about 400 feet up the moorside and then ran to the north along the side of the moor, roughly on the level, to Bagden Quarry about three-quarters of a mile away.

Little is known about the history of this line. It was owned by Henry Heys and Co. who also owned some other quarries further up the valley. The tramway probably opened soon after 1870, the year in which the railway from Rochdale as far as Facit, just north of Whitworth was opened. The tramway is shown on the Ordnance Survey map of 1890 but has no rails indicated on the map of 1909 survey. This seems to confirm what elderly residents told B. Roberts, namely, that the quarry and therefore, of course, the tramway closed down some time around 1900. There is mention of a line serving a certain 'Home Rule Quarry', though there remains uncertainty as to its site. It may well be just another name for the quarry at Bagden.

The only engine known to have worked on the Bagden Line was an 0-4-0 tank (probably saddle) engine called 'James' built by Black Hawthorn. On the closure of the tramway it was sold to Brooks and Brooks for use on their Cloughfold to Ding tramway.

The Walk

[1] From the entrance descend into Healey Dell on the wide tarmac road until you get near the impressive viaduct that once carried the Rochdale to Bacup line of the Lancashire and Yorkshire Railway over the dell. Take the path that leads off to the left in front of the viaduct and which gives access to the top of it. Cross over the viaduct and continue northwards on the well made up path on the former railway trackbed.

[2] After passing through a cutting you pass the remains of Broadley Station where there was a loop but only one platform. Another cutting follows at the end of which, just after passing under a wooden footbridge, a wide flat space is reached.

[3] This is the site of Broadley Sidings where the stone from Bagden Quarry, after having been cut and dressed, was loaded into standard gauge railway wagons.

Turn left and follow the track which heads off across the flat area to the west, aiming for a point just to the left of the red brick factory building ahead. The track you are on is that of a former three foot gauge tramway which ran up to Spring Mill ahead. Apparently not only did cloth come down the line but vats of acid for bleaching and coal for the engine at the mill went up the line so it was, presumably, a powered type incline. The Spring Mill tramway is later than the Bagden Quarries tramway and does not appear on a map of 1890 survey as the latter does.

After the track bears a little to the right, a stream is crossed and the climb up the former short incline to mill follows. At the top, just before

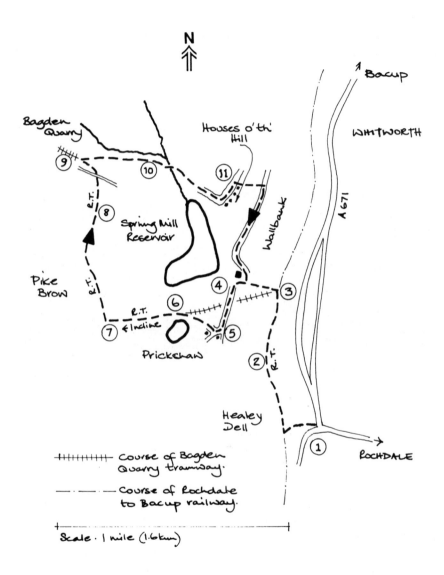

the factory gate, turn left onto the well used trackway that crosses the course of the mill tramway.

A glance to the south, across the little valley you have climbed out of, will reveal a good view of the Bagden Quarries tramway climbing, partly on an embankment, diagonally up the slope on the other side.

Well up on the open moor the course of the tramroad aims for its isolated goal, Bagden Quarry.

[4] Continue along the trackway as it bends to the south, round a large brick shed on the left, to cross the valley. The track, which is now stone flagged, then runs southwards and uphill between two stone walls.

On your right, just past the end of the well made waterworks boundary wall, there is a large bulge in the wall. It was here that the Bagden tramway crossed over the trackway on a bridge. A few paces further on look back and you will have a good view of the course of the tramway as it runs westwards on a well made embankment, aiming for the steeper part of the hillside ahead.

[5] Continue on the trackway until, next to a stone building, another

trackway joins it on the right. Turn right and go along this other trackway for about 50 yards until you reach the first house in the hamlet of Prickshaw.

Here turn right onto the rougher trackway that comes in on your right on the east side of the houses. After passing through a metal gate the trackway turns into a sunken lane which can be a bit wet at times. On your right a good view is to be had of the Bagden tramway's former incline climbing uphill on a well made embankment.

[6] Conditions underfoot improve and then a wooden gate, situated on the tramway trackbed, gives access to the open moor at the foot of the steep part of the incline. The crossing loop at the halfway point of the incline was situated just to the east of this gate.

Go straight up the hillside to the west on the trackbed of the former incline.

[7] At the top, as is usually the way with inclines, the trackbed very suddenly levels out and you find yourself on a small level platform cut out in the hillside. A stone lined channel can be seen running west to east in the middle of the platform. Perhaps this once carried metal rods from a brakes man's hut to the balancing wheel or drum which would have been situated somewhere near the back of the platform and round which the wire rope of the incline would have been wound. Probably, as is usually the case in Rossendale, the balancing wheel would have been placed on a vertical axle. Looking downhill, on a clear day at any rate, you can see full length of the tramway so far covered.

From the incline top the tramway took a course to the north roughly following the contour until Bagden Quarry, about three-quarters of a mile further on, was reached. Make your way north on the trackbed of this section which is clear and easy to follow.

After about 300 yards, on your left, you pass the remains of some small coal pits. Evidence on the ground suggests that these may have been once connected with the railway.

[8] Further on, after passing through a shallow cutting, the course of the tramway goes through a gap in a stone wall. As the gap is filled with water and barbed wire it is necessary to climb to a little to the left and cross over the rather tumbled stone wall on what appears once to have been a stile. Continue on to the north proceeding along the tramway

embankment making for the north west corner of the field.

Here the tramway crosses on the level an old way named on maps 'Broad Lane'. Cross over this lane and continue following the trackbed of the tramway as it bends to the north west through a cutting.

At the end of the cutting, on your right, are the remains of a stone building which may well have been an engine shed. Evidence on the ground seems to indicate that it was linked to the tramway. Ahead lies journey's end for the tramway, namely, Bagden Quarry. Ian Goldthorpe in his book on the Rossendale Way rightly says that 'Bagden Quarry looks as though it closed suddenly one day leaving everything just where it was. There are piles of roofing flags neatly stacked, but never taken away ... also piles of kerbstones.' The layout of the tramway at the quarry face during the last phase of the quarry's existence is also clear.

The suggested route back is along the Rossendale Way which crosses the tramway trackbed at the south east end of the quarry and then drops diagonally down the slope to the north of the course of the tramway immediately to the east of the last mound of waste from the quarry. Continue downhill until you are just level with the tops of the large beech trees which fill the ravine or clough below (do not attempt to cross down into the clough) and then proceed to the east along the path which runs along the edge of the clough.

[10] Almost level with the last of the beech trees on your left, the path joins an old cart way which takes you down the slope via a hairpin bend to a ford. Cross over the stile on the other side of the ford and then bear right to join, after just a few yards, a well used farm trackway which leads off to the south east.

After a gentle climb, with views of Spring Mill Reservoir on your right, the quaintly named 'Houses o' th' Hill' come into view. At the junction of the trackways turn left and proceed north eastwards along the trackway with the houses to the right. After the last house on the right leave the trackway by taking the path which goes off on your right through a wooden door set in a stone wall.

[11] The path passes by the north side of the house and then joins a private tarmac road which it follows until the road bends to the right. Here the path leaves the road and continues straight on down the hill to the right of a stone wall. At the bottom of the field turn right onto the

trackway that goes off to the south west running between estate houses on the left and fields on the right.

After about 400 yards the houses end the red brick buildings of Spring Mill, passed earlier in the walk, come into view. From here you have a good view of the bottom section of the Bagden tramway's trackbed as it runs downhill to the exchange sidings at Broadly. Continue on the trackway as it winds round the east of the works building until you reach the point where you joined it on the way out, namely, at the top of the incline of the former tramway to Spring Mill. From here you can make your way back to the start of the walk by the same way you came out.

Index